NEIL
LENNON

NOTES ON A SEASON

NEIL
LENNON

NOTES ON A SEASON

Reach Sport

www.reachsport.com

First published in Great Britain in 2020 by
Reach Sport, 5 St Paul's Square, Liverpool, L3 9SJ.

www.reachsport.com
@reach_sport

Reach Sport is a part of Reach plc.
One Canada Square, Canary Wharf, London, E15 5AP.

ISBN: 978-1-911613-81-7

Photographic acknowledgements:
SNS Images.

Printed and bound by CPI Group (UK) Ltd,
Croydon, CR0 4YY.

NOTES ON A SEASON

2019-20

'I'M HONOURED TO BE CELTIC MANAGER AS WE EMBARK ON OUR BID FOR A HISTORY-MAKING TENTH LEAGUE TITLE IN A ROW'

Foreword

To be the Celtic manager who has led the club to nine league titles in a row is something that I'm very proud of. Every year, our top priority is win the league, and that is a tough challenge, with every team wanting to beat the champions. The fact that we have been able to achieve this goal for the past nine seasons is testament to the hard work and dedication of everyone at the club, throughout every single one of those nine campaigns.

It also means that we have replicated the historic achievement of Jock Stein's legendary Celtic side who were the first to do so, back in the 1960s and '70s.

I'm often reminded that, at the end of the 2010/11 season, amidst the disappointment of not winning the title, I spoke at Celtic Park following our final league game and told our supporters that this wasn't the end, it was only the beginning.

It wasn't that I had a crystal ball and could look into the future. I believed it because I looked at our squad, I looked at the set-up behind the scenes, I looked round at sixty thousand Celtic supporters there that day and I knew the potential here and what we were capable of achieving.

I'm also proud to have started this exceptional run by winning those first three titles, and that has been added to with the achievements of both Ronny and Brendan, who have also played a huge part in this era of success that Celtic is enjoying.

It was a dream come true for me to return to the club as manager in February 2019, and we have since added two further league titles to take our tally to the nine.

The players, of course, deserve enormous credit for delivering this run of titles. In my first spell, I was lucky enough to work with some great professionals, and this has been the same again since I returned to Celtic.

I can't speak highly enough of the players – their attitude and application on the training pitch every single day and, of course, the quality of their performances on a matchday. It has been a real joy to work with them and I have loved watching the team throughout this season.

We've played a brand of attacking and, at times, swashbuckling football that I believe is in the best traditions of this football club, and we have entertained while also winning along the way. Football is a team game, of course, and every member of the squad plays their part, no matter how much game-time they get over the course of the campaign. However, I'm sure none of the players will mind me singling out Scott Brown and James Forrest for particular praise, given that they have both been at Celtic for every one of the nine in a row triumphs.

I have said it on many occasions and I will say it again here. Scott and James are modern-day Celtic greats, and we've been lucky to have them at our club over the past few years. They are very different in character but equally important to our cause.

Scott is our captain and our leader, on and off the park. He was my captain when I first took over as Celtic manager back in 2010, and he has continued to set the standards every day as to what is expected of a Celtic player. He is a fantastic example to any aspiring footballer through his dedication, his professionalism, his desire to win and his qualities as a player, which are many.

While Billy McNeill will always be rightly considered our greatest ever captain, Scott is a truly great Celtic captain.

With James, I'm delighted at the way his career has developed over the years. I gave him his first-team debut back in May 2010, having worked with him previously in the reserves and seen first-hand what a talent he was.

He has gone on to show just how talented he is, and he has been an integral part of the club's nine in a row run. He is obviously a great success story for our Youth Academy, while the way he has dedicated himself to his profession is a wonderful example to every player at whatever stage of their career they're at. James continues to get better with each passing season, and it's a real joy to work with him.

It is, of course, for our supporters that we work hard every day and every season. We want to deliver success to them as they're an integral part of everything we do. The backing they give us, week in week out, home and away is incredible and it really is one of our greatest strengths. It is something that everyone at the club genuinely appreciates and I want to thank all of our fans for the tremendous support they've given the team. The forthcoming season will, at least initially, be unusual and unprecedented in that we will kick off the campaign playing games behind closed doors. The priority of everyone at the club has always been, first and foremost, the safety of all our supporters, but we hope that it won't be too long before Celtic Park is full of fans once again, who can give us the backing that they are renowned throughout the game for.

Season 2020/21 will be an absolutely vital one for all of us, and I am truly honoured to be the Celtic manager as we embark on our bid for a history-making tenth league title in a row.

While I know that this is what is exciting the fans, and they have been singing about it for a long time now, my job, and that of my backroom staff, will be to manage the pressure of this season and ensure that the players focus only on the next game that's in front of them.

That's an approach I've spoken about on many occasions because it's one that has served us well up to now, and it's one that we will continue throughout the campaign. We have to meet each challenge as it arises and not think too far ahead as to what may or may not happen. We will all work hard every single day and do everything we can to ensure that the forthcoming season truly is one to remember.

The Notes on a Season book, of course, tells the story of our nine in a row campaign through my programme notes from each of our home games and also the weekly interview I have with the club's official magazine, the *Celtic View*.

While we are all looking forward to the season ahead, it's also good to look back at what we've achieved and this is exactly what this book does. After all, Celtic supporters sing about knowing our history, and winning nine league titles in a row is now a memorable part of our incredible history.

It was an unprecedented end to the season but no one could argue that, having established a 13-point lead and with just eight games remaining, we are not worthy champions. We thoroughly deserve this title and it's something that the whole Celtic Family should be proud of.

I hope you enjoy, through the pages of this book, looking back over an incredible campaign and that it also whets your appetite for the season ahead.

Neil Lennon
Manager
Celtic Football Club

JUN– JUL

2019

Pre-season was an important time for Neil Lennon's side, with the manager preparing for vital Champions League qualifiers.

26th June: v SC Pinkafeld (F) A
29th June: v Wiener SC (F) A
2nd July: v FC St Gallen (F) A
9th July: v FK Sarajevo (UCL) A
13th July: Rennes (F) H
17th July: FK Sarajevo (UCL) H
24th July: Nomme Kalju FC (UCL) H
30th July: v Nomme Kalju FC (UCL) A

'I'M REALLY PLEASED WITH THE CONDITION THE BOYS ARE IN. THE WORK WE'VE DONE IS THE BEST WE COULD HAVE HOPED FOR'

Pre-season

Celtic reported back for pre-season in the last week in the last week of June, with the squad heading off to Austria for their training camp. Following a number of pre-season games, the Hoops were immediately into competitive action, with UEFA Champions League qualifiers in early July.

And in his first interview of the 2019/20 season with the *Celtic View*, Neil Lennon reflected on a positive pre-season and some of the new additions to the squad.

On the benefits of the training camp

It's been a very successful pre-season trip. We got a lot of good work in during the 10 days and we're pretty much injury-free, although we'll need to check how Bayo is because he felt a twinge after the second game. I'm really pleased with the condition the boys are in and I was really pleased with the performances as well. I've got nothing but positive things to say about the attitude of the players and the backroom staff. Everyone involved in this trip has worked very hard.

The work we've done is the best we could have hoped for. In terms of fitness levels in a short space of time, I think they look good. We toned it down slightly when we came back to Glasgow and focused more on some football technical work.

On the striking options in the squad

It was an outstanding performance from the young boys

(against Austrian side SC Pinkafeld). There were some great performances and some great goals. I was really pleased with the control of the game as well.

Obviously Mikey Johnston sets it all off. He's been the catalyst for a lot of good things, whether that's been in training or the games.

For such a young team to play so well was very encouraging.

The pathway's there. It's just up to the players now to go and take it. The experienced players are great role models for the younger guys and a great motivation for them as well.

We want to develop our own, and the experience that some of these younger guys will have taken from this trip will hopefully stand them in good stead as the season goes on.

It was a good goal from Bayo (v SC Wiener) and a really good finish. What pleased me was the quality of chances we created, even in the first half without scoring.

Bayo missed a couple of chances before taking his hardest chance with a left foot finish. We'll have to wait and see how he is because he felt a little twinge in his hamstring and he was looking really good as well. On top of that Mikey, along with James and Odsonne, came through the game really well.

Leigh Griffiths got his customary goal. It's good

to see him back and getting the goals. No matter the opposition, to score quality goals like that shows that he's a quality player and a quality finisher. It's just pure instinct really and he knows he needs to get a little bit fitter.

He's come a long way in a short space of time so we're delighted with not only having him back but the contribution he's making as well.

We had a big squad and we didn't want the players to get 15 minutes against St Gallen because it wouldn't have benefited them that much. What we decided to do was split the squad and have two games, one against the development team and the other against the St Gallen first-team.

For the senior boys it was important to get more minutes in their legs. You can get as much out of training as you like, but in terms of match fitness it is crucial at this stage.

The likes of Bitton, Griffiths, Sinclair and Christie were involved in that game. Myself and John Kennedy wanted to get them football minutes in their legs and that sets them up nicely. Regardless of the opposition, their attitude was brilliant. It was very hot at that time of day. They felt tired at the end but that's exactly what they needed.

With the boys who played 90 minutes in the last game against St Gallen, they had to work really, really hard towards the end with us being down to 10 men after Jozo was sent off.

But even if we hadn't been, we're at altitude a little bit, with us being 800 meters up. They worked hard, particularly in the last 15 or 20 minutes and that will set them up for the next couple of weeks.

On the arrival of Christopher Jullien at Celtic

I'm delighted to have Christopher Jullien here now. He's been a target for the club now for quite a while. He has great attributes and has played at a very high level now for the last couple of years.

He's one of those players whose career has progressed forward all the time. When I met him, you could see his enthusiasm and hunger there to come and play for Celtic.

The fact that his wife's Welsh will help him come and settle into a different culture very quickly, but, as a player, he has all the attributes we're looking for.

Luca Connell's a very talented young player. He broke into the senior side with Bolton in the Championship. We've had a good look at him, have had good reports and he was away with the Irish senior squad training. The reports came back positive and we liked the look of him.

UEFA Champions League
First qualifying round, first leg
Tuesday, July 9, 2019
Asim Ferhatović Stadium
Sarajevo, Bosnia

FK Sarajevo 1, Celtic 3

Goals: Johnston (35), Edouard (51), Sinclair (84).

Line-up: Bain; Ajer, Simunovic, Bitton, Bolingoli (Hayes 56); Brown, McGregor, Forrest (Sinclair 78), Christie, Johnston (Morgan 64); Edouard. Subs not used: Gordon, Ralston, Julien, Hayes, Griffiths.

Neil Lennon spoke to the *Celtic View* between the two legs of the UEFA Champions League qualifier against FK Sarajevo, having seen his side establish a commanding first leg led in Bosnia.

And the Celtic manager stressed the importance to the club of having a positive European campaign.

On his Euro ambitions for Celtic
I want this club to be competing on the big stage. The Champions League is a Blue Riband event. I don't want to over-talk it because you can end up with egg on your face, but that's what we want, that's what we're trying to do here. Whether we can do it or not, time

will tell. We might need a little bit of luck in the games, perhaps a little bit of luck with the draw as well, but we'll give everything we have on and off the pitch to make it happen.

Our whole focus and concentration at the minute is to get through the Sarajevo tie and then see what the second round brings. We know who we could get there, so, all going well, our focus will shift to that, and it's imperative that we can give ourselves every chance of qualifying.

I'm obviously very pleased with the first-leg result and it's given us a good foothold in the tie even if we still have a bit of work to do. I'm delighted with the three away goals and we'll build on that. The week in between the games gets them a little bit sharper, a little fitter, and so we'll be expecting even more from them on Wednesday night.

The Rennes game last weekend was also a good workout and a chance for some of the players to get up to speed. But there's still a lot of work to be done, in terms of the physical fitness and match sharpness. In the short space of time that we've been here, though, it's gone very well so far. It's a fair point that players might take a little less time to get up to speed, but you always worry about mental and physical fatigue, and given the short space of time they have off, it catches up with them.

On the challenges of early season competitive games

It's just a question of trying to balance the squad in between games, give them enough rest and recovery and still get the hard work into them as well. It's a big ask.

You're talking eight games before you can play in the Champions League, and we know each one and each leg is fraught with danger and risk.

The big European nights, the big Champions League nights, are essential for the players, the fans, the club itself. It's a difficult path nowadays, but once you're in there it's great, it's a free hit, but we're doing the hard yards first. Each game has its own difficulties, whether that be travel, different cultures of football, you could come up against opposition who are already midway through their season, so we just have to take it one tie at a time.

I just want to keep building on the success we've had. As I've said before, there won't be sweeping changes here. There will be changes to the personnel, but that's only natural at a football club, there will be changes every season.

We want to bring in quality players and we have our own objectives. The treble again might be on the horizon, but it's a difficult thing to do. In the main, what we want to do, first and foremost, is qualify for the

Champions League. Our priority is to win the league after that.

Lewis Morgan has looked sharp, fit, he's well-balanced and I like the way he can manipulate the ball with both feet. He's quick across the ground, and what he'll be looking for now is the end product, whether that be an assist, or a goal himself. Players who can do a good job, not an average one, in one or two positions, is always vital. What we don't want is these players to be a jack of all trades but masters of none, we want them to be exceptionally good in any position that we play them.

We've had a few of those over the years, in terms of players that you can rely on to play a number of positions, and while we don't want to overcook that, if it's needs must at times, it's good to be able to rely on these guys. If you look at Kristoffer Ajer, for example, he played right-back on Wednesday and looked great. That's a big bonus to have in the squad.

I know the talent that Mikey Johnston has, and we want more from him now. People say it's a big year for him – it is, because it's the next one. Every season is going to be important and big for Mikey. He's a talent, and he's unquestionably got the game to play for us at a consistent level, and we've been delighted with the way he looked in pre-season and with the start he gave us in Sarajevo as well. It augurs well for him.

v FK Sarajevo
First qualifying round, second leg
Wednesday, July 17th, Celtic Park

'EVEN IN THESE EARLY STAGES, IT'S CLEAR THAT THE STANDARD OF THE TEAMS IS VERY STRONG'

UEFA Champions League

GOOD evening and welcome to Celtic Park for tonight's UEFA Champions League qualifier against FK Sarajevo, and I also want to welcome our visitors from Bosnia and Herzegovina to our city and our stadium.

It's our first competitive home game of the new season, and we want to start with a positive result. The aim, of course, is to book our place in the next round of the competition, and we got a good result in the first leg last week.

Despite conceding the opening goal, I thought the players responded very well and certainly from when we equalised, I thought we controlled the game.

We scored three good goals on the night, and it's always pleasing to get goals away from home in Europe, so we're set up nicely to complete the job tonight.

However, there are still 90 minutes ahead of us and we will not be complacent or underestimate FK Sarajevo. They showed from the first leg that they are a very competitive team who are dangerous on the break, so we will be focused on the task ahead and determined to finish the job.

Even in these early qualifying stages of the UEFA Champions League, it's clear that the standard of the teams is very strong and so we know, should we progress, that we face several more difficult ties.

However, it is a challenge that we are looking forward

to, and our target is to progress through these qualifying rounds.

Saturday's friendly against Rennes was a valuable one in terms of our European preparations. Even though it is early in their pre-season preparations, you could tell they are a quality side who move the ball about the pitch and close down very quickly.

I thought we did well, and it was good for a lot of the players to get some valuable game-time. We were also able to give Chris Jullien and Luca Connell their first starts, and it was great for both of them to experience playing at Celtic Park.

Thanks, as always, for your support. It's one of our greatest strengths and I know that, in the months ahead, you'll give the team the backing that we need and always appreciate. Enjoy the game.

Celtic 2, FK Sarajevo 1

Goals: Christie (25), McGregor (76).

Line-up: Bain; Ajer, Bitton, Simunovic, Bolingoli; Brown, McGregor, Christie (Henderson 88), Forrest, Morgan (Sinclair 86); Edouard (Griffiths 79). Subs not used: Gordon Jullien, Ralston, Hayes.

Neil Lennon

v Nomme Kalju
Second qualifying round, first leg
Wednesday, July 24th, Celtic Park

'CONFIDENCE IS HIGH IN THE SQUAD BUT OUR FOCUS IS ON TAKING IT ONE GAME AT A TIME'

UEFA Champions League

GOOD evening and welcome to Celtic Park for tonight's UEFA Champions League tie against Nomme Kalju, and I would like to extend that welcome to our visitors from Estonia.

These ties come around so quickly following on from the previous round, but we have been preparing well over the past week since our game with FK Sarajevo, and we're all looking forward to tonight's match.

We had two good performances in the last round in what were our first two competitive games of the season, and that has also proved beneficial in terms of the overall fitness of the squad, with the players getting valuable game-time.

We hope that will stand us in good stead over the two legs of this tie, here tonight at Celtic Park and then next Tuesday in Estonia.

Nomme Kalju are halfway through their domestic season, and they will make things difficult for us. They had a great result in North Macedonia to get through the last round, so we know they will be tough opponents.

However, confidence is high in the squad and we're determined to do everything we can to ensure we're in the third qualifying round of the competition.

The draw for that was made earlier this week, so we know that should we get past Nomme Kalju, we face a trip to either Romania or Israel. However, our focus is always on taking it one game at a time. That has been a key element in our success here over the past few years, so we will be looking no further ahead than tonight's match at Celtic Park.

I have said many times before, and will no doubt do so many times in the future, but our supporters can and do play a key role for the team. Home and away, the backing you give the players is incredible, and we will need that again tonight as we look to get a positive result and take a lead with us to Estonia next week. Enjoy the game.

Celtic 5, Nomme Kalju 0

Goals: Ajer (37), Christie (44 pen, 65), Griffiths (45+3), McGregor (77).

Line-up: Bain; Simunovic, Bitton, Ajer; Brown, Forrest, Christie (Ntcham 70), McGregor, Bolingoli (Christie 38); Griffiths (Morgan 59), Edouard. Subs not used: Gordon, Jullien, Sinclair, Hayes, Morgan, Johnston.

Post-match notes

Leigh Griffiths was delighted to score on his first start after taking a few months out of the game. 'I can't score goals without my team-mates', he said, 'so the biggest thanks go to them. Without them, the manager, the coaching staff and everybody connected with the club, I wouldn't be back on the pitch.'

UEFA Champions League
Second qualifying round, second leg
Tuesday, July 30, 2019
The A.Le Coq Arena, Tallinn, Estonia

Nomme Kalju 0, Celtic 2

Goals: Kulinitis (10 og), Shved (90+3).

Line-up: Gordon; Ralston, Simunovic, Jullien, Bolingoli; Brown, Bitton (Shved 70), Morgan, Ntcham (Christie 84), Johnston (Sinclair 61); Griffiths. Subs not used: Bain, Ajer, Hayes, Edouard.

Neil Lennon's post-match reaction: 'We had good control over the course of the game, and we scored another great goal towards the end. I thought we could have had a few more, but I can't ask any more than what the players are giving me at the minute. We know we're going to get stiffer examinations moving forward, we understand that. But for where we are, we're not getting carried away, 7-0 over two ties is very appetising. That's very impressive, I have to say. We were anxious to get Marian Shved some game-time tonight and you could see what the goal meant to him from a personal point of view. You have to remember how young he is, and it'll take him some time to settle into a new culture. That goal is a great start to his Celtic career.'

AUG

2019

**Neil Lennon's side kicked off the campaign
to win a ninth consecutive league title with
a magnificent seven in their opening game,
but there were mixed fortunes for Celtic on
the European stage.**

3rd: v St Johnstone (SPFL) H
7th: v CFR Cluj (UCL) A
10th: v Motherwell (SPFL) A
13th: v CFR Cluj (UCL) H
17th: v Dunfermline (LC) H
22nd: v AIK Solna (UEL) H
25th: v Hearts (SPFL) H
29th: v AIK Solna (UEL) A

Neil Lennon

v St Johnstone
Saturday, August 3rd, 3pm

'THE PLAYERS WILL HAVE TO FOCUS AS WE LOOK TO GET OUR LEAGUE CAMPAIGN OFF TO A WINNING START'

Premiership

GOOD afternoon and welcome to Celtic Park for what is always a very special occasion. Flag Day at Paradise is a great way to kick off the new Premiership season, and it's something that everyone has enjoyed in recent years.

It's a way to acknowledge the achievements of the previous season, and enjoy a moment of celebration before we begin anew, hoping to emulate those achievements in the campaign ahead.

The players here have done an incredible job over the past few years, and to have achieved the Treble Treble last season is truly remarkable. They deserve all the praise and plaudits that have come their way.

Today, too, will be an emotional one as Liz McNeill and Sadie Chalmers are our guests of honour who will unfurl the league flag just before kick-off.

Our thoughts, as always, are with them and their families as they continue to mourn the loss of Billy and Stevie. We do, too, though we know they will never be forgotten for everything they did for our football club.

It's a great gesture by the club to invite Liz and Sadie to be central to the pre-match ceremony and I know that they will receive the warmest of welcomes when they step on to the pitch.

For the players, they will also have to focus on the 90 minutes ahead as we look to get our Premiership campaign off to a winning start.

We face a tough opponent in St Johnstone, and I

know that Tommy will have his team well-organised and determined to frustrate us. He has, over a number of years now, done a brilliant job there and, as always, his team won't make it easy for us.

We go into today's game full of confidence, however, after several good European performances, the most recent of which was the win over in Estonia last week.

That sets us up for another tough tie, with the first leg in Romania this Wednesday. However, the preparation for that will only begin after the final whistle today.

For now, our focus is solely on our opening league game and ensuring we deliver a positive response.

It's going to be a packed stadium today and I know you will all enjoy the Flag Day celebrations as much as us. Let's hope the celebrations will continue throughout the afternoon. Enjoy the game.

Celtic 7, St Johnstone 0

*Goals: Johnston 9, Christie 26, 30, 68, Ntcham 73,
Edouard 80, Griffiths 87*

*Line-up: Bain; Elhamed (Ralston 50), Bitton, Ajer, Bolingoli; Brown,
McGregor, Forrest, Christie (Ntcham 71), Johnston (Griffiths 76);
Edouard. Subs not used: Gordon, Sinclair, Hayes, Morgan.*

Post-match notes

The 7-0 victory was Celtic's biggest ever win over St Johnstone, eclipsing the two previous 6-0 victories over the Perth side, in 1937 and 2018.

Speaking to the *Celtic View* after the game, Neil Lennon expressed his delight at the opening day league win.

On the Flag Day win

It was great to see the goalscorers also get their assists, and it was great to have so many different goalscorers in the first place. I loved the last three goals in particular, and there were some great contributions from the subs. There was some real variety in our play in attack and the players really went out and expressed themselves in the right way.

There was also good intelligence about the way they played. There was good sharpness and a good tempo. Sometimes with that, though, you can get bogged down with it. We didn't do that on Saturday, and there weren't any periods of the game where we let St Johnstone get a foothold on things. That pleases me.

The pressure we applied to St Johnstone was relentless, and the players and the fans got a real buzz out of playing that way. It's not going to be like that every week, but it's a great start to the season. I was delighted, not only with the goals, but also the clean sheet.

On his half-time team talk

I told them to go out and win the second-half. It's always difficult to come in with such a big margin and do the same in the second period. To be fair, the reception the players got at half-time from the supporters was amazing. I said, 'Look, you've deserved that, but it's a two-way street – you've got to entertain the fans'. If you're doing that and they're responding the right way, it just shows you what can happen. It's always difficult to pick yourself up after a 15-minute break, you come in off a high and it can be difficult to get going again.

To their credit, in the last 20 minutes to half-an-hour, they really turned on the power again. You could see St Johnstone were tiring and the players exploited the gaps. We're not going to win 7-0 every week, but the mentality of the team and their approach to the game was very positive.

On Hatem Elhamed's Celtic debut

Hatem had a great debut, and I think he set the tone for the game. He was strong, he was very quick and able going forward, and he was comfortable on the ball. He's also a good size, so aerially, for a full-back, he's in a good place as well. He can be delighted with his contribution. Unfortunately, he picked up a bit of a dead leg, but we're hoping he can be fit for Wednesday.

It was a bit of a happy coincidence being able to play Hatem alongside Nir, a player who he already knows. Kris seems to be comfortable to play on the left side of the centre-half position, and while it's not ideal to have to play Nir in there, it shows what a quality player he is when he steps in there and looks as comfortable as he does.

UEFA Champions League
Third qualifying round, first leg
Wednesday, August 7, 2019
Dr Constantin Radulescu Stadium,
Cluj, Romania

CFR Cluj 1, Celtic 1

Goal: Forrest (37).

Line-up: Bain, Elhamed (Bitton 87), Simunovic (Jullien 74), Ajer, Bolingoli; Brown, McGregor, Christie; Forrest, Edouard, Morgan (Ntcham 66). Subs not used: Gordon, Griffiths, Hayes, Shved.

Neil Lennon's post-match reaction: 'We've got to be delighted with the away goal. I was delighted with our attacking intent, and I thought we defended resolutely throughout the game as well. You have to give Cluj credit, they scored a fine goal on the counter-attack, but our reaction was superb, with Christie and Edouard playing brilliantly throughout the game. And, of course, James Forrest is a big-game player and he's popped up with another crucial goal for us. We've got a big game to negotiate on Saturday. It's a quick turnaround, we hope to get a good result there and we can then look forward to the second leg next week. Over the last couple of games at Celtic Park, we've been on incredible form. Next week, we'll need the crowd, and then the players need to go out and perform.'

**Scottish Premiership,
Saturday, August 10, 2019,
Fir Park, Motherwell**

Motherwell 2, Celtic 5

*Goals: Ajer (15), Griffiths (41), Forrest (67),
Edouard (77), Christie (86 pen).*

*Line-up: Bain; Ajer, Bitton, Jullien, Bolingoli; Brown, McGregor,
Forrest (Christie 67), Ntcham (Sinclair 79), Morgan; Griffiths
(Edouard 62). Subs not used: Gordon, Hayes, Shved, Bayo.*

Neil Lennon was delighted with another high-scoring performance from his team, as he told the *Celtic View* following the victory at Fir Park. And there was praise for a number of his players.

On Kristoffer Ajer's goalscoring contribution

Kris has been outstanding at right-back during the games we've played him there. That quick response comes from the team.

When you pull things level so quickly, we don't have time to affect much of the play in that short window. That comes down to the individuals. We started off the game pretty passively, but once we found our aggression and purpose, we were in control more or less until the final whistle.

I'm obviously disappointed conceding a goal in the manner in which we did, but we responded brilliantly. From there on, we really turned on the power in both attack and defence. We had good legs in midfield, we looked a real threat and we could have had a couple more, but to score five at Fir Park, at any stage of the season, that's no mean feat. Doing so off the back of arriving home so late on Thursday morning and only having a day's recovery, that's a pretty remarkable turnout.

It's a really good trait to have, to be able to show character and not lose track of what you want to do.

Last weekend, it was more or less an immediate response, which you don't always get.

It was a great team goal too, a lovely ball from Jamesy and a great finish from a player who's slap bang on-form. Kris has the capability of adding to his goal tally, on top of everything else he brings to his game.

His whole make-up as a player – his athleticism, his pace, his reading of the game, it's all there at the moment. To add a goal on top of that will always be a huge bonus for us.

On Nir Bitton's return to action
Nir brings that calmness to the backline, that control, that level-headedness – all on top of everything else he brings to the game.

He's obviously got height on his side as well, and that's always something which is good to have at centre-half. He reads the game very well, which is a great trait to have when playing in that area, and it's also the quality that they bring to those areas. That's true versatility. It's not just an ordinary player going in there, filling in a position. They're also weighing in with a very important contribution.

We're all pleased for Nir, we're pleased that he's made a full recovery and that he's getting more game-time. He's very popular among the players, and he is in his last year of contract, so this is an important year for him.

For him, it's important that he stays as healthy as he possibly can, and makes his contributions to the team, like he's been doing so well so far. I see him more as a midfield player, ideally, but with the way things have been – considering injuries and suspensions – he's played very, very well at centre-half.

On the form of his attacking players

James Forrest is in a great place, he's had a great three or four years and that's possibly because he's now coming into his peak.

He knows his body now, he knows what recovery is required, and he looks after himself very well away from football. His play is so dynamic, there's a real intelligence about his game, he sees things very quickly and he's a great finisher once he's in there. He's got a great mentality towards the game and long may that continue.

We talk about Jamesy as if he's a veteran of the game, but we need to remember he's only just turned 28. But to consider the career he's had so far... people would give their right arm for everything he's achieved so far.

Ryan Christie has had a great start to the campaign. He's brimming with confidence, he converted the penalty last weekend, and continues to be outstanding. There's so much to his game, and I'm sure there's so much more to come.

He's in a great place and if he stays fit I'm sure he'll have another monumental season. It's early days yet, but I've been delighted with his application and the way he approaches games.

He sees things very quickly and, evidently, he has goals in him. His energy levels are terrific, but not only that, he's a terrific footballer.

Post-match notes

Kris Ajer's goal — the first of five Celtic scored at Fir Park — was also his first against Scottish opposition. The Norwegian had previously scored against FK Suduva and Nomme Kalju. He would go on net goals against Aberdeen and Kilmarnock later in the campaign.

Neil Lennon

v CFR Cluj
Third qualifying round, second leg
Tuesday, August 13, 2019, Celtic Park

'THERE ARE FEW BETTER PLACES THAN CELTIC PARK ON A EUROPEAN NIGHT'

UEFA Champions League

GOOD evening and welcome to Celtic Park for tonight's UEFA Champions League qualifying match against CFR Cluj. I also want to extend that welcome to our visitors from Romania.

Last week's first leg was a tough match, and we were pleased to score an away goal and come away with a 1-1 draw.

However, we saw throughout that game just how difficult Cluj are as a team, and I'm sure that will be the case again tonight. Both sides know that a place in the play-off round is at stake, so it is a massive game and it's one that we're looking forward to.

We go into the match full of confidence following Saturday's victory over Motherwell. It's always tough to come back to domestic action following an away European tie, and the fact that we were playing at midday after arriving back in the early hours of Thursday morning made it even more challenging.

However, I thought that the players responded magnificently and, after a tough start when Motherwell made it difficult for us, we really dominated and scored five goals. It was very enjoyable to watch, and it has continued our good start to the Premiership season.

Since then, of course, we have focused on tonight and preparing to take on a Cluj side who also enjoyed a good league result at the weekend.

We're playing at home, which is always a very positive

thing, and with our support behind us, we'll go out determined to get a good result.

I know it's been said many times in the past, and will no doubt be said again in the future, but there are few better places than Celtic Park on a European night.

Enjoy the game.

Celtic 3, CFR Cluj 4

Goals: Forrest (50), Edouard (61), Christie (74).
CFR Cluj win 5-4 on aggregate

Line-up: Bain; Simunovic, Brown (Bayo 87), Christie, Johnston (Morgan 73), Ntcham (Griffiths 83), Edouard, Elhamed, Ajer, McGregor, Forrest. Subs not used: Gordon, Jullien, Bitton, Bolingoli.

Neil Lennon's post-match reaction: 'In the first half we were so passive. We weren't physical enough, and all the nuts and bolts of the game weren't there. We got a warning beforehand and then lost the goal when we did the exact same thing again. After half-time, we got the right response, but we shot ourselves in the foot with the goals we conceded. We had the lead twice and threw it away.

'We need to regroup and make sure we qualify for the Europa League. We all wanted Champions League football and we've only ourselves to blame for not getting that. We've been loose, and in the important moments of the game, we switched off. The players are bitterly disappointed, and we accept blame as a collective.'

v Dunfermline Athletic
Saturday, August 17th, 3pm

'IT'S THE START OF OUR DEFENCE OF THE TROPHY WE'VE WON FOR THE PAST THREE SEASONS'

League Cup

GOOD afternoon and welcome to Celtic Park for today's Betfred Cup match against Dunfermline. It's the start of our defence of a trophy that we've won for the past three seasons, so it goes without saying that we want to get that defence off to a successful start.

We're facing a Dunfermline side who have started the season well, and we'll have to be aware of the threat they can pose in this tie.

Stevie Crawford's side came through their group, beating St Mirren in Paisley along the way, and scoring plenty of goals, so they will come here full of confidence.

However, we've also been scoring with frequency since the start of the season, so we'll be looking to add to our goals tally this afternoon.

There's no doubt that everyone – players, management and supporters – is very disappointed after Tuesday night's game. We didn't perform well in the first half and were punished accordingly.

However, the players showed a great response after the break, and we looked dangerous whenever we were on the attack.

We had the lead twice and threw it away, and we shot ourselves in the foot with the goals we lost. As I said, we're all very disappointed to have gone out of the Champions League, and we accept the criticism that comes our way.

Now, though, we have to regroup and make sure that we qualify for the Europa League. We've got two vital play-off ties, starting this Thursday night, and we'll be determined to do everything we can to ensure we make it into the group stages.

The focus on that game, however, will only begin after today's Betfred Cup match. It's important that we are ready for the challenge ahead over the next 90 minutes, and our only aim is to ensure that we are in the draw for the last eight of the competition. Enjoy the game.

Celtic 2, Dunfermline Athletic 1

Goals: Johnston (54), Forrest (114).

Line-up: Gordon; Elhamed, Jullien, Ajer (Ntcham 75); Bitton, Bolingoli (Hayes 95), Johnston (Morgan 115), McGregor, Christie; Griffiths (Forrest 55), Edouard. Subs not used: Hazard, Bayo, Shved.

Neil Lennon was delighted that his players returned to winning ways against Dunfermline after their Champions League exit, as he told the *Celtic View.*

On beating Dunfermline in the League Cup
The players responded brilliantly at the weekend to get the win. It wasn't easy but they got there and that's important. They weren't at their best but they showed their winning mentality and they can draw on that in the upcoming games when the going gets tough. We've had no issues with our attacking play. I'm not a big stats man but I was happy to see we had 36 shots and 11 on target in the game against Dunfermline. That's one stat I do care about.

We've had seven different goalscorers so far this season so we have goals in us. We just need to make sure we keep them out at the other end.

On Mikey Johnston's goal

I thought Mikey was outstanding. He had a really, really good performance against Dunfermline. He's showing that consistency we're looking for and if he can keep doing that, he's going to have a good season. We scored two very good goals in the game, Mikey had a big performance and Jamesy is a big-game player. When we need important goals, he seems to come up with them, and he's done that many, many times. With him, it's not luck, it's not a coincidence, and he proved to be the match-winner again against Dunfermline.

On the challenge of domestic football after Euro ties

I'm delighted that we're in the next round and I'm delighted with the character and patience the players showed. They've come through a really stiff test of character, a real examination, and they've come through the other side. They won't see it the way I see it. I played in a great Celtic side and we had days like that. I remember a penalty shoot-out against Partick Thistle that went to 10-8 or something like that and they were a Championship team at the time. We've come through a tough examination physiologically rather than a football one.

v AIK Solna
Play-off round, first leg
Thursday, August 22, 2019, Celtic Park

'ATTACKING AND GOING FOR GOALS IS THE CELTIC WAY, AND WHAT THE FANS EXPECT'

UEFA Europa League

WELCOME once more to Celtic Park where the games are coming thick and fast at the moment, and, come the weekend, we will have played three games here in three different competitions over the course of little more than a week.

That started with Dunfermline in the League Cup on Saturday and will end with Hearts in the league on Sunday, but tonight it's all about AIK of Stockholm in the UEFA Europa League and we know how difficult this will be against a side with a strong Swedish pedigree.

So a warm welcome to Celtic Park goes to all the players, staff and supporters of AIK tonight, as Rikard Norling brings his side here as Swedish champions and, like us, they will be more than keen to progress from this play-off to the group stages.

Winning the Swedish title is no mean feat, as we just have to look at the many Swedes who became heroes at Celtic Park to know the quality of footballer the country produces.

However, we are intent on delivering a positive result tonight to take to Stockholm for next week's second leg, and we go into this game with a positive attitude as the group stages are within touching distance and we want to ensure that we are there for the draw.

We know that the backing of the supporters at Celtic Park tonight will go a long way to help us achieve that aim, and every fan here this evening will play a part in Celtic progressing in the tournament. The team go into the game on the back of a difficult, but ultimately successful League Cup tie against Dunfermline as our winning mentality showed under testing circumstances.

We only scored twice in that match, but the team have been scoring freely, both domestically and in Europe, and the fact that our goals have come from seven different scorers around the pitch proves that we have that attacking edge to us.

The aim is obviously to shore things up at the other end of the pitch while still going for goals up front, which is the Celtic way and what the fans expect.

We hope that's what we can deliver tonight against AIK and I hope that you can play your part in driving us on to those aims. Enjoy the game.

Celtic 2, AIK Solna 1

Goals: Forrest (48), Edouard (72).

Line-up: Gordon; Bolingoli, Jullien, Simunovic, Ajer; Brown, McGregor, Forrest (Ntcham 82), Christie, Johnston (Morgan 82); Edouard (Bayo 84). Subs not used: Hazard, Hayes, Bitton, Griffith.

Neil Lennon's post-match reaction: 'It was an outstanding performance, and a great team performance. We played well in the first-half, but I thought we were magnificent in the second. Some of the football we played was great and we scored some fantastic goals. Odsonne is playing brilliantly. He's leading the line superbly, and I can't speak highly enough of his talent. He's an integral part and important figure in this team. I also think James is underplayed in terms of public image, but I think that suits him. That's five goals in five games for him now and we never take that for granted. He's an outstanding player and he's got so much more to come. I've known him for a long time. He did wonders for me the first time round and he's doing it again.

'We defended resolutely and strongly. AIK were tough, but I thought we played very well and had good energy around the pitch and a spark that we might have lacked last weekend. Next week is a European tie away from home against the Swedish champions. We've given ourselves a foothold which is important, but we need to see it through next week.

'Boli was good, as was Christopher, and Kris Ajer is having an outstanding period at the moment. We didn't give AIK a foothold in the game early on, we pressed as a unit and the tempo pleased me. We've now got a big game at the weekend, but we want to get the job done properly next week. We still have an important 90 minutes ahead of us.'

Post-match notes

Celtic have never lost a home match against Swedish opposition, having beaten Helsingborgs (2013), Elfsborg (2013) and Malmo (2015) at Paradise. Only Malmo managed to score, netting twice in a 3-2 defeat, courtesy of former Celtic striker, Jo-Inge Berget.

v Hearts
Sunday, August 25th, 3pm

'THE BACKING AND SUPPORT OF THE CELTIC PARK CROWD IS ONE OF OUR GREATEST STRENGTHS'

Premiership

GOOD afternoon and welcome to Celtic Park for today's Premiership match against Hearts. It's our third league match of the new campaign and we're aiming to continue our good record, having won the previous two fixtures, against St Johnstone and Motherwell.

Due to the production deadlines for today's programme, I had to pen these notes ahead of Thursday night's Europa League tie against Swedish side, AIK, but it goes without saying that I hope we're going into today's match on the back of a positive result.

We have a big match coming up on Thursday, with our return leg in Stockholm, and our focus from tomorrow will be on that. However, over the past few days our preparations have been solely on today's game against Hearts. While Craig's team will be disappointed with their opening two league results, they had a great win over Motherwell in the League Cup last week, at a difficult venue and in terrible weather conditions. So they will come here full of confidence and determined to get something from the game. We know that they are always tough opponents, so we will have to be at our best today in order to enjoy a successful 90 minutes.

It's our fourth home game in a row and, as always, it's great to play at home with the Celtic Park crowd giving the team much-needed backing. We all appreciate the commitment that our fans give in order to support the team, and it's one of our greatest strengths.

Today, our focus is on the Premiership and on doing everything we can to try and make it three wins out of three in our campaign. Enjoy the game.

Celtic 3, Hearts 1

Goals: Berra (og 29), McGregor (54), Bayo (59).

Line-up: Forster; Ajer (Ralston 87), Jullien, Bitton, Bolingoli; Brown, McGregor, Ntcham (Johnston 69), Forrest, Christie, Bayo (Griffiths 78). Subs not used: Gordon, Hayes, Shved, Edouard.

Neil Lennon's post-match reaction: I thought the three goals against Hearts were fantastically created and fantastically taken. We had a lot of nice one-two stuff, good early crosses, and I'm delighted with that. The early switches of play were also really important in breaking Hearts down because they were very narrow and congested in the midfield. The variation of our play was excellent, and the quality of our passing was superb. It really opened Hearts up, it stretched them and it allowed us to get in behind them.

'I'm sure Bayo's performance meant a lot to him. He's had to be really patient and he's had a frustrating period with injuries – his hamstring injury in March, and the recurrence of that he picked up in pre-season, when he looked good on the training pitch – so he's had to bide his time. Before the Hearts game, we told him not to put himself under any unnecessary pressure, that he's not on trial but he should go out and try and be free and show everyone what he's good at. After a bit of a slow start, he came on to a very good game, and I'm delighted with his contribution.'

UEFA Europa League
Play-off round, second leg
Thursday, August 29, 2019
Friends Arena, Stockholm

AIK Solna 1, Celtic 4

Goals: Forrest (17), Johnston (34), Jullien (87), Morgan (90+2).

Line-up: Gordon; Ajer (Ralston 15), Jullien, Bitton, Bolingoli; Brown, McGregor, Forrest, Christie, Johnston (Morgan 70); Edouard (Bayo 76). Subs not used: Hazard, Hayes, Hayes, Griffiths.

Celtic's comprehensive victory in Sweden to book their place in the group stages of the UEFA Europa League delighted Neil Lennon.

And as he told the *Celtic View*, his team were now looking forward to the European challenges ahead.

On the display in Sweden

It was an outstanding performance. The whole team were outstanding. The subs that came on made a contribution and I couldn't have envisioned us playing so well. Going forward, we were a dream at times. Scoring four goals away from home, it could've been more. It was brilliant. We looked strong and played brilliant football at times, defended resolutely when we needed to.

I can't ask for any more from the players at the minute. Apart from one half against Cluj we've made an outstanding start to the season, and we've now got some big games to look forward to.

The first goal was a beautiful goal. There was great interplay from James and Odsonne and then a composed finish. I thought Jamesy was magnificent, on and off the ball. The front four looked very powerful and looked a threat. We kept going and kept wanting more goals. There was a real thirst for goals tonight and that's the way we want to play.

We looked at the first half against Cluj and that wasn't us. Ever since then we've tried to step-up the tempo of our pressing. John and Damien do great work with that and we're seeing the results of that, and the more they get used to the hard work, the easier the hard work becomes.

It was an outstanding performance from start to finish. We scored four away from home in Europe, we haven't done that for a long, long time and the quality of the goals was excellent.

The quality of the performance was excellent and it was a pressure game obviously, but the players handled it brilliantly. We beat a very good side comprehensively over two legs, so there is a lot to be positive about.

On the players' contribution

Browny was outstanding and is really back to his best again, and Callum has just been so consistent over the piece. But the front players really excited us. Odsonne Edouard is in great form, Ryan Christie has been outstanding and James Forrest is great to watch when he's playing like that. His goal was sublime and his all-round game was really high quality.

I've been excited throughout the majority of the season. There's been a bit of negativity about the place, you can understand that to a certain degree but, when you're scoring goals at a very fast rate, then we're very positive and there's a lot to be happy about.

On the Europa League group-stage draw

It's a great draw. There's a couple of glamour games there and a chance to maybe exact some sort of retribution on Cluj as well, so we're delighted to be in there and delighted with the group. There are a lot of big games to look forward to, which is exactly what we want.

Lazio is a great draw, it's very glamorous and it's a trip to Rome as well, I think that's something everyone here will look forward to. I feel we've got the making of a good side. I'm not going to make predictions, but I think that we can make a good impact on the group. After playing Cluj recently, that would be the first thing that would probably come into the players' heads, and with Lazio and Rennes, we'll think we can have a real go at both of those teams.

SEP

2019

The first Glasgow derby of the season saw Celtic record an emphatic victory at Ibrox, while Neil Lennon guided his side to an impressive draw away to Rennes in the UEFA Europa League.

1st: v Rangers (SPFL) A
14th: v Hamilton (SPFL) A
19th: v Rennes (UEL) A
22nd: v Kilmarnock (SPFL) H
25th: v Partick Thistle (LC) H
28th: v Hibernian (SPFL) A

Scottish Premiership,
Sunday, September 1, 2019,
Ibrox, Glasgow

Rangers 0, Celtic 2

Goals: Edouard (32), Hayes (90).

Line-up: Forster; Elhamed, Bitton (Bauer 66) Jullien, Bolingoli; McGregor, Brown, Christie, Forrest (Ntcham 66), Johnston (Hayes 84), Edouard. Subs not used: Gordon, Morgan, Bayo, Griffiths.

The first Glasgow derby of the 2019/20 saw Celtic travel across the city to Ibrox and produce a dominant performance to win 2-0.

Speaking to the *Celtic View*, Neil Lennon spoke of his pride in his players' performance in what was a thoroughly deserved victory.

On the pre-match hype for the home side
We were an afterthought coming into the fixture. It was all about the opposition and what they were going to do to us. We didn't listen to any of it. We stayed strong and played brilliantly. We came here to win, we came here to be strong.

Everyone wrote us off. Bookies had Rangers as favourites, but we proved we're still going to have a big say in this title race. We were very motivated, hungry and had great belief about us. You can't listen to the noise surrounding the game, you have to stick to what you believe in. I have a great backroom team and we set our stall out to be competitive.

I can't speak highly enough of the players, they were absolutely brilliant. I couldn't have asked for anything more. It was a perfect performance with really hard, professional football with quality.

People will always have doubts the longer this run goes on, but the character this team has is huge. Some of them have great leadership qualities. Off the top of your head, Scott Brown comes to everyone's thinking. Callum McGregor and James Forrest, without being vociferous, lead by example.

I think they like people writing them off and it serves as added motivation for them, not that they need it, because their focus and work ethic is second to none. We're only four games into the season and there'll be ups and downs as we go along, but we've made a fantastic start.

On the team's tactical approach

We took the game to Rangers and dominated the start of the game. Everyone might have laughed at the kick-off, but we wanted to play in their half which we didn't do in the corresponding fixture when we conceded a free-kick and were a goal down early on. There are many ways to skin a cat. This is a derby, it's competitive and you have to fight fire with fire. You have to quieten the crowd and we did that to perfection.

From my own experience, you have to press with aggression sometimes. For this fixture, we felt it was the right way to go about business. In the first half we bossed it. Brown, Bolingoli and Jullien had outstanding performances and I have a front four who are a handful for any team.

We deserved to win the game by more. The second goal was the icing on the cake. We defended strongly when we needed to. Elhamed had a brilliant performance coming in from the cold. The personality, character and strength of the team was evident when everyone had written us off. We're very proud, we take the three points and psychologically it's a good win for us and we move on.

On the performance of the players

The defence were brilliant. The mentality was so good. Christopher Jullien took on a real leadership role. Nir Bitton has been exemplary in that position, he was outstanding. Hatem was a concern going into the game, but he played the occasion and the game brilliantly. Boli's had his detractors, but they're becoming fewer and fewer now. He's becoming more consistent and again had a really strong game going forward and defensively. Moritz came on and did a very steady job in difficult circumstances. Their mentality, as well as their ability, shone and that's given me a lot of satisfaction and confidence with them.

Since I've come in the door in February, Odsonne's been brilliant and he's still young. His improvement's been rapid and his all-round game's getting better. If you wanted anyone to be in a one-on-one situation at Ibrox, it's him. He has that great temperament and mentality to stay really calm and unflustered. His footwork at times is dazzling and he's so live and athletic. He's getting stronger too, his aerial challenges were good at Ibrox and his hold-up play was great, so he's deceptive in that way. He does things that other players can't do. His reverse ball for Boli for example was top class. There's a great understanding between him and all the attacking players. You could see that against AIK last week with him and James.

The two of them are very quiet. James takes everything in but doesn't give much away. Odsonne's very similar. One of the staff summed it up best when they said he talks to you with his eyes. There's a great understanding between the two of them.

Post-match notes

At one point in the game at Ibrox, Celtic's entire back four were all derby debutants — Moritz Bauer, Hatem Elhamed, Chris Jullien and Boli Bolingoli.

Scottish Premiership, Saturday, September 14, 2019, New Douglas Park

Hamilton Accies 0, Celtic 1

Goal: Forrest (4).

Line-up: Forster; Bolingoli, Jullien, Ajer, Elhamed; Brown, McGregor, Elyounoussi (Rogic 67), Forrest, Christie; Edouard (Bayo 77).
Subs not used: Gordon, Bauer, Hayes, Ntcham, Griffithss.

Neil Lennon's post-match reaction: 'I'm delighted, we dominated the game from start to finish. Obviously when you get the early goal you're thinking it could be more but I thought first half we were outstanding at times. In the second half we hit the bar and you always need that second goal to put a gloss on the scoreline and reflect the performance. The pitch was very dry and sticky which made it difficult to play the kind of flowing football we want to play, so it's a brilliant win, an absolutely brilliant win off the back of a two-week break. That's five wins out of five in the league and I've been told that's the first time that's happened in a while so you can see how difficult that is to do.'

UEFA Europa League, Matchday One, Group E, Thursday, September 19, 2019, Stade de la Route de Lorient

Rennes 1, Celtic 1

Goal: Christie (58 pen).

Line-up: Forster, Elhamed, Ajer, Jullien, Bolingoli (Hayes 69), Brown, McGregor, Forrest, Christie, Elyounoussi (Ntcham 56) Edouard (Bayo 84). Subs not used: Gordon, Bauer, Morgan, Rogic.

Celtic kicked off their UEFA Europa League group-stage campaign with an away game against French side, Rennes.

Neil Lennon was pleased with the performance, his only disappointment being that the Hoops didn't bring all three points home, as he told the *Celtic View*.

On the team's mentality

We were disappointed to go a goal down because we had good control of the game. I said to the boys at half-time, are you going to play and lose? Are we going back to that mentality? The reaction in the second half was very good and we saw the game out quite comfortably despite some bizarre refereeing decisions.

Looking at us first half the two midfield boys, Brown and McGregor were really good. Chris Jullien had a great game and defensively we looked solid. It didn't feel like we were in any trouble and then the penalty went against us. That's just something Kris has to work on a little bit but the rest of his game was outstanding.

It was a clear penalty. Ryan's got there first and the centre-half's taken him out in the box. We feel really hard done by that and then Bayo's second yellow card is farcical. There's minimal contact across the goalkeeper's midriff and he's gone down clutching his face.

The referee looks like he was playing on and then decided to change his mind. Bayo had every right to go for the ball and in the end he's actually tried to jump out of the way. We feel hard done by in that circumstance and Bayo's distraught but he has our full support.

The players showed great concentration and discipline. I'm really proud of them and pleased with the result. We're on great form and the mentality of the team is really good at the minute.

On playing against a top side on the European stage

The overall performance and the control we had for long periods of the game against one of the top teams in France away from home was fantastic. There was a maturity and quality about our performance. My only tinge of disappointment was that we didn't win the game, because the performance certainly merited at least a point.

With the experience we've got now, the players are adapting to it. I didn't want them to play well and lose, and they showed great desire to come back into the game. At stages we looked like we were going to go and win it.

We dealt with most of Rennes' play very well. Our play was of very high quality, but it's just one performance and we know the group is wide open. We now look forward to a home game where we have to try and take maximum points from that.

Rennes are a team that beat PSG a few weeks ago comfortably. It's a good result and a good fillip for the players and gives them belief that they can go on and make strides in the group.

They looked comfortable in that environment, with no panic about us being a goal down and they had a good reaction. That's what I'm getting from this team a lot.

In moments of adversity, they find something more and there's a good belief from them that they could've got something from the game.

What pleased me more than anything was the control we had in the game. My two guys in midfield, Scott Brown and Callum McGregor, as a partnership were fantastic.

Neil Lennon

v Kilmarnock
Sunday, September 22nd, 1pm

'I'VE BEEN DELIGHTED WITH THE DISPLAYS OF THE TEAM DURING OUR MARVELLOUS START TO THE SEASON'

Premiership

September 2019

WELCOME to today's game as we aim to maintain our 100 per cent start to the SPFL campaign against a Kilmarnock side who have been on a good run lately, so we know the visitors will equally be looking to keep up their winning form.

A lot has happened since our last home game nearly a month ago when we beat Hearts 3-1. In the intervening weeks there has, of course, been the international break but we also had the culmination of the transfer window and we now have our full complement of 11 new signings.

Also, on the pitch, we kept up the winning sequence by qualifying for the group stages of the UEFA Europa League, winning the derby match 2-0 at Ibrox and then defeating Hamilton Accies 1-0 last weekend at New Douglas Park.

That was followed up by our European trip and, due to production deadlines, I'm writing these programme notes before our game against Stade Rennais in France, and I hope that we come into today's match on the back of a positive result in the Europa League.

The first half at Hamilton saw some outstanding football from the side and the early goal gave us the game. Another goal or two would have been more reflective of the play and the possession we had, but I'm delighted that we recorded five wins in our first five SPFL matches.

Our form recently shows that the new men are adapting to the game here, and I've been delighted with the displays of the team in general during our marvellous start to the season and we aim to keep that up this afternoon for the visit of Kilmarnock.

They didn't have the best of starts to the season, but over the past few games they have returned to the form that they've shown over the past couple of seasons, and Angelo's experience in the game is a big part of that.

We know we are in for a tough test this afternoon as Kilmarnock have been keeping it tight at the back as well as winning games, but this is a good game for us to come back to following our European trip.

So we hope that we will all be celebrating another win when the final whistle blows and then we can start concentrating on the visit of Partick Thistle this midweek in the League Cup. Enjoy the game.

Celtic 3, Kilmarnock 1

Goals: Edouard (44, 53), Christie (57)

Line-up: Fraser, Bauer (Elhamed 79), Ajer, Jullien (Rogic 84), Bolingoli; Brown, McGregor, Ntcham (Hayes 74) , Christie, Forrest; Edouard. Subs not used: Gordon, Taylor, Elyounoussi, Bayo.

Neil Lennon's post-match reaction: 'I thought it was a really good performance. We were effervescent, played with a good tempo and showed intent to attack and score goals against a good side who are on form. That came off the back of the really good performance against Rennes. It's difficult to maintain that tempo and standard with a two-day recovery and an early kick-off. Sometimes those games can be a bit dry and stale because the players can be a bit stiff and rusty, but I thought the players were excellent and the atmosphere at the game was great as well.

'Their keeper made a lot of good saves. There was a chance from Ollie Ntcham just after half-time which I thought was destined for the top corner, but he made a great save. We had 14 attempts on goal and I'm not big on stats, but that is one I'm interested in to see if we are creating and breaking the opposition down in the right way. There was no panic at half-time. We deserved to be in front, but you can't allow luck or any other element to get in the way and, to be fair, I thought we played some brilliant football.

'I'm getting everything I want from this team. We're working the goalkeeper and we're creating lots of chances. I'm so happy with Odsonne and Ryan. They deserve everything they. Forrest was outstanding today and was a real catalyst for a lot of good things. Ntcham had a great game and all-round we looked a very competent side to the point my goalkeeper saved a penalty. Bauer came in and had an excellent debut and Bolingoli had a great assist for the second goal. He played well and had good energy about him. The two centre-halves played really good as well. I'm not getting carried away, it was a big ask to come back from a demanding game in midweek and put on a great performance but they've done it in spectacular style.'

Neil Lennon

v Partick Thistle
Quarter-final
Wednesday, September 25, 7.45pm

'WE'VE ENJOYED SUCCESS IN THIS COMPETITION AND IT'S SOMETHING WE'D CLEARLY LIKE TO REPLICATE'

League Cup

GOOD evening and welcome to Celtic Park for our Betfred League Cup quarter-final against Partick Thistle. I also want to extend that welcome to our visitors from across the city.

This is an important game for us and it's one that we're all looking forward to.

We've enjoyed tremendous success in this competition in recent years, winning the trophy for the past three seasons, and it's something that we'd clearly like to replicate again this season.

The aim at this club is to try and win every competition we enter, and that obviously includes the Betfred League Cup.

The success of previous campaigns has been built on preparing well for each cup-tie, and our focus since the weekend has been on tonight's game.

I thought the players produced an excellent performance against Kilmarnock on Sunday, and we want to produce something similar tonight in order to ensure that we're in the draw for the semi-final.

However, we know that Partick Thistle will come here equally determined to achieve the same thing. They are now under new management, and I wish Ian McCall all the best in his new job, though obviously I hope he doesn't get off to a winning start tonight!

We know that we go into this game as favourites to win, being the cup holders and also having home advantage, but there will be no complacency within our squad.

Cup competitions can always provide shocks and surprises, and Partick Thistle will come here looking to deliver a cup shock, with their players wanting to impress their new manager.

So we will be ready for whatever this cup-tie brings up, and we go into the game full of confidence. The players will also receive the customary great backing from our supporters who, as always, were magnificent on Sunday.

I thought the atmosphere was great in that game, and I'm sure it will be the same again tonight as we look to deliver a positive result. Enjoy the game.

Celtic 5, Partick Thistle 0

Goals: Bayo (14), Rogic (46), Ntcham (56, 63), Sinclair (76).

Line-up: Gordon, Frimpong (Hendry 78), Elhamed, Ajer, Hayes, McGregor (Brown 62), Ntcham, Rogic, Morgan, Bayo, Elyounoussi (Sinclair 66). Subs not used: Forster, Edouard, Bolongoli, Forrest.

Post-match notes

Jeremie Frimpong made his Celtic debut against Partick Thistle, and Neil Lennon said of the 18-year-old: 'As soon as we brought him in, he's excelled. For a guy with a small stature he has lot of personality, energy and strength. We feel he could be a really good player here.'

Scottish Premiership,
Saturday, September 28, 2019,
Easter Road, Edinburgh

Hibernian 1, Celtic 1

Goal: Christie (23).

Line-up: Forster; Bolingoli, Ajer, Jullien, Bauer; Brown, McGregor, Ntcham (Hayes 60), Christie, Forrest (Sinclair 84); Edouard (Bayo 71). Subs not used: Gordon, Elhamed, Elyounoussi, Rogic.

Neil Lennon's post-match reaction: 'I'm not going to criticise the team. Their desire, physicality and quality of play, in the main, was very good. It was a good performance and we've made a tremendous start to the season. While I'm not here to criticise referees, we should have had two clear-cut penalties. I thought we dominated the game. We looked a little bit flat in the final third on occasion and then the subs gave us a real good burst of energy in the final 20 minutes but our finishing let us down. We're not going to win every game. We're not going to blow teams away in every game. There's an expectation before the game but I don't always expect us to win. I believe we can and I want us to win. We need to take the luck element out of it. Hibs got the luck with the goal and we showed a good reaction after that to go and get the equaliser. Our finishing and that snap in the final third for some reason wasn't there today.'

OCT

2019

While Celtic's domestic form remained impressive, it was results in Europe which particularly pleased the manager, with home wins over CFR Cluj and Italian giants, Lazio.

3rd: v CFR Cluj (UEL) H
6th: v Livingston (SPFL) A
19th: v Ross County (SPFL) H
24th: v Lazio (UEL) H
27th: v Aberdeen (SPFL) A
30th: v St Mirren (SPFL) H

Neil Lennon

v CFR Cluj
Matchday Two, Group E
Tuesday, October 3rd, 8pm

'THE NEW PLAYERS CAN PLAY THEIR PART IN MAKING IT A NIGHT TO REMEMBER'

UEFA Europa League

GOOD evening and welcome to Celtic Park for tonight's UEFA Europa League match against CFR Cluj, and I would also like to welcome our opponents from Romania, who are making their second visit to Glasgow this season.

It was certainly an eventful game back in August when we last met, although it was ultimately disappointing for ourselves as it was Cluj who won the game and the tie.

However, the way the players have responded since then has been excellent, and having qualified for the group stages of the UEFA Europa League, we began this stage of the competition with an excellent performance and result away to Rennes. Indeed, I felt that our display merited all three points, and we showed, against one of the top sides in the French league, that we can compete at this level. Now, we want to follow that up with all three points in our first home game of the group stages.

We're already familiar with the Cluj squad and the dangers they will pose, and they also got their UEFA Europa League campaign off to a successful start with an impressive home win over Lazio. So they will come here full of confidence, and we know we will have to be at our best if we want to be successful tonight.

Confidence is also high within our squad. We've had a very good start to the season, the team has been playing well and we're looking forward to playing in front of our own fans tonight.

European nights at Celtic Park are always special occasions. I've been lucky enough to experience plenty of them as a player and manager, and I'm sure this game against Cluj is going to be another great occasion under the lights.

It will also be an experience to enjoy for the players who've just joined the club in recent months. I know they will all have heard just how special our stadium can be, and they will hopefully play their part in making it a night to remember.

It's going to be a packed stadium, and your support on these occasions is absolutely vital. The backing we get from our fans is always one of our greatest strengths, and I know you will play your part as we look to get an important victory tonight. Enjoy the game.

Celtic 2, CFR Cluj 0

Goals: Edouard (20), Elyounoussi (59)

Line-up: Forster; Elhamed, Jullien, Ajer, Bolingoli; Brown, McGregor, Elyounoussi, Forrest (Hayes 84), Christie (Ntcham 88); Edouard. Subs not used: Gordon, Bauer, Bitton, Sinclair, Rogic.

Neil Lennon's post-match reaction: 'From a European point of view, our form has been absolutely excellent so far without getting carried away. The Europa League, perhaps with the amount of money swirling about down south, maybe doesn't hold that much prestige but for a lot of other countries, and big countries in Europe, it is still a prestigious competition. For us, with the history that we've had in Europe since the Lisbon Lions, I think the fans crave it and it's important when players come here, to not only do well domestically, but also enhance the club's reputation in Europe as well. That's what we're trying to do.

'I was excited before the game – just being back as Celtic manager on that stage and in that arena. It's very, very special on European nights and the players responded brilliantly to the atmosphere too. You want to make Celtic Park a really difficult place for opposition teams to come, and the players are doing that. What they got on Thursday night was a real experience of what it can really be like in terms of atmosphere and authenticity of a big stadium and the rawness in the air. You can almost smell the big-game atmosphere and they reacted to that very well.

'I said that to the players afterwards that I think we've got the makings of a good side. It's embryonic in the season, we know that and we're not getting carried away, but I'm absolutely thrilled and I'm delighted for the supporters as well – to see European football here with a great performance from the team, which was exciting, and with a lot of chances created. We're only two games in so, for me, the group is still wide open. We still have to play Lazio, which will be very difficult, but we've given ourselves a foothold in the group, nothing more.'

Post-match notes

Mohamed Elyounoussi scored his first goal for Celtic in this game – one of seven he would net for the Hoops in the 2019/20 season.

Scottish Premiership,
Sunday, October 6, 2019,
Tony Macaroni Stadium, Livingston

Livingston 2, Celtic 0

Line-up: Forester, Bauer, Jullien, Ajer, Bolingoli (Hayes 73); Brown (Ntcham 75), McGregor, Forrest (Bayo 55), Elyounoussi, Edouard. Subs not used: Gordon, Elhamed, Bitton, Sinclair.

Neil Lennon's post-match reaction: 'We put a lot into Thursday and then we had to play a long time with 10 men as well so that might have come into it. I was hoping for a bit of a reaction from the subs as well but they didn't really affect the game as well as we would have liked. I thought we started well, looked lively and had a couple of chances early on. We had decent control of the game up until the red card. I'm expecting better. I said to them beforehand that this game was a concern. It's a dangerous opponent and dangerous environment, with an opponent who would be up for it, so we had to match that.'

Post-match notes

Celtic suffered their first domestic defeat of the season away to Livingston, while Ryan Christie's red card was the only one the team received in the Premiership in the course of the campaign.

v Ross County
Saturday, October 19, 3pm

'OUR FOCUS HAS TO BE ON MAKING A QUICK RETURN TO WINNING WAYS'

Premiership

GOOD afternoon and welcome to Celtic Park for today's Premiership match with Ross County, and I would like to extend that welcome to our visitors.

It's good to be back home and it's a game we're all looking forward to. As always, we're determined to do everything we can to win, but given our most recent two league results on the road against Hibernian and Livingston, it's important that we return to winning ways.

Certainly, that's our focus and that's what we've been preparing for over these past two weeks.

Obviously, with the latest round of international fixtures, many of our players have been away representing their respective countries, so it has only been over the past few days that we've been able to get the full squad together again.

That is something we're used to, however, and is a sign of the quality within our squad that so many players are selected for international duty.

As Celtic manager, of course, my main concern is that all of our players report back injury-free, particularly given the heavy schedule of games that lie ahead between now and the winter break at the end of the year.

Ross County will come here full of confidence following their strong start to the season. They did very well to bounce straight back up to the Premiership, and they have done well so far, sitting in the top half of the table.

So we are well aware of the potential threat they pose to us today. It means that we will have to be at our best in order to ensure a successful afternoon, and as recent league results have shown, there are no easy games in this league.

Confidence is high within our squad, however, and the players are looking forward to the 90 minutes ahead.

As always, the backing from our supporters is absolutely vital for us. That bond between the players and the fans is so important and can help us, not only today, but in every game we play. So let's hope that, together, we can deliver all three points this afternoon. Enjoy the game.

Celtic 6, Ross County 0

Goals: Elyounoussi (3, 71), Edouard (46, 50),
McGregor (48), Forrest (55).

Line-up: Forster, Frimpong, Jullien, Ajer, Bolingoli; Brown, Rogic,
McGregor (Bitton 75) Forrest (Shved 75), Edouard (Bayo 65),
Elyounoussi. Subs not used: Gordon, Bauer, Hayes, Elhamed.

Neil Lennon's post-match reaction: 'For me, the highlight of the win was the performance, regardless of what happened in the other games at the weekend. From start to finish it was the best complete performance, certainly in my time here in my second spell.

'To score six is no mean feat and it could have been more. It was really controlled, quick and exciting football. I thought we played better in the first half but we scored the deluge of goals in the second half. Some of the football in the first half was breathtaking, and that was against Ross County who had come off the back of four games unbeaten, so it shows the measure of the performance. I said to my staff that we would only get one minute of time added on, because the game was wrapped up and very flat. We made three substitutions and Ross County made three so that's three minutes. It may have come in handy to have had another couple of minutes for us to add one or two more.

'But the overriding emotion for me was one of immense pride in that performance. Jeremie Frimpong had a great performance against Ross County and we're really pleased with what we're seeing of him. I hope he'll go on to progress into the player we believe he can be. What you see on the pitch is what you see off the pitch. He's this energetic buzzbomb who's all personality and is really proud to be here. In the week leading into the Ross County game, his training levels were outstanding and it was impossible to leave him out of the game.'

Post-match notes

Celtic's impressive 6-0 victory over Ross County came on the 62nd anniversary of the club's famous 7-1 victory against Rangers in the 1957 League Cup final at Hampden, which remains the biggest ever margin of victory in a UK domestic cup final.

October 2019

v Lazio
Matchday Three, Group E
Thursday, October 24, 8pm

'THIS TEAM THRIVES ON THE ATMOSPHERE OUR FANS CREATE HERE AT PARADISE'

UEFA Europa League

GOOD evening and welcome to Celtic Park for tonight's UEFA Europa League game against Lazio, and I would also like to extend that welcome to the players, management and supporters of Lazio who have made the journey from Rome to Glasgow.

European nights here are always great occasions and ones that we all look forward to, and to play host to one of the top names in Italian football just makes the night all the more special.

We're pleased with the start we've made to our group-stage campaign, with a draw away to Rennes and then the victory here over Cluj.

The players produced good performances in both of those games, and that augurs well for the remaining fixtures. Our next two ties, of course, are as hard as they come, with this double-header against Lazio.

In two weeks' time, we'll head to Rome to play in the Stadio Olimpico, but tonight we're at Celtic Park, in front of a sell-out crowd, and we're determined to do everything we can to enjoy another positive result.

Confidence is high within the squad, not least following Saturday's impressive performance here against Ross County. That was the best display by the team since I've returned to the club, and is also right up there alongside the best in both of my spells as manager. We want to take that form into tonight's game, though we're under no illusions as to how difficult our opponents are.

Simone Inzaghi's side bounced back from their defeat against Cluj on matchday one to beat Rennes in their last UEFA Europa League match. And at the weekend, they showed their character as a team, fighting back from 3-0 down to draw 3-3 against a very good Atalanta side.

So we will have to be at our best tonight if we want to get anything from this game. Of course, we hope home advantage will play its part.

This match is completely sold out, and I know our fans will generate an incredible atmosphere to help drive the players on. This is what the team thrives on, it's one of our greatest strengths and, together, hopefully we can ensure it's another special European night at Paradise. Enjoy the game.

Celtic 2, Lazio 1

Goals: Christie (67), Jullien (89).

Line-up: Forster; Elhamed (Bitton 83), Ajer, Jullien, Bolingoli (Hayes 85); Brown, McGregor, Elyounoussi (Rogic 65), Forrest, Christie; Edouard. Subs not used: Gordon, Bauer, Sinclair, Bayo.

Neil Lennon was delighted with the 2-1 victory over Lazio at Paradise, and reflected on the magnitude of the win when he spoke to the *Celtic View*.

On beating a top-class European side
It's so important to win your home games. That, to

me, was a Champions League game tonight, with the quality on show from both sides and the tempo the game was played at. Lazio came to really play, so for us to get on the positive side of the result is fantastic. We have seven points now, but there's still a lot of work in the group to ensure we qualify.

Lazio were superb, and they had periods in the game they were the better team. We started the game very well and then the psychology of the game changed. Lazio scored and they got the upper hand. We made a change to get more support up to Odsonne and thankfully that worked.

To go toe-to-toe with Lazio and come away with the three points is a huge shot in the arm for the team, and it's a very proud night for everyone associated with the club.

I'm more proud of the resilience that they've shown, and I'm proud of the win. At times we could've handled aspects of the game better but that's me being pedantic looking for the perfect performance all the time – you're not going to get that. When you put it into context, we've just beaten Lazio 2-1 at home and it's an amazing feeling.

On the goalscoring and goalkeeping heroes

At his age, Christopher's got his best years in front of him now. I think that, since he's come in and settled, he's been absolutely outstanding. There's no doubt he can improve and he can take his game on – and there is that willingness to do that. His professionalism is fantastic and his attitude since he's come in through the door has been brilliant, as has his will to win.

He has to control his emotions sometimes, but over the piece, he's been immense and I thought he was outstanding against Lazio. That goal and that performance should give him a real shot in the arm going forward.

At times against a quality team, you need your goalkeeper to play well and Fraser pulled off two outstanding saves. The players got more energy and chances and got the winner. It's been an epic night for the players and the club. I know what Fraser's capable of and he's starting to show that. He makes saves other goalkeepers can't make. The block from Parolo was a brilliant save, too. You saw the two world-class saves he made. That's why we brought him in. You need your goalkeeper in big games to perform and he's certainly adapted to that.

Post-match notes

Lazio were actually the first Italian team to play in Scotland when they took on Celtic at Paradise in September 1950. The friendly match saw the Hoops beat Lazio 4-0, with John McPhail scoring all four of Celtic's goals.

**Scottish Premiership,
Sunday, October 27, 2019,
Pittodrie, Aberdeen**

Aberdeen 0, Celtic 4

Goals: Edouard (11), Frimpong (15), Forrest (37), Elyounoussi (44).

*Line-up: Forster: Frimpomg, Julien (Bitton 45), Ajer, Bolingoli; Brown,
McGregor, Rogic, Forrest, Elyounoussi (Hayes 81): Edouard
(Bayo 70). Subs not used: Gordon, Elhamed, Bauer, Sinclair.*

Celtic followed up their stunning victory over Lazio
with a tough trip to Pittodrie to take on Aberdeen, and
in a blistering first-half performance, the Hoops scored
four goals without reply.

Neil Lennon was, not surprisingly, delighted with the
performance and the 4-0 victory for his side, when he
sat down to talk to the *Celtic View*.

On an impressive domestic display

I'm delighted with the reaction and the recovery of the
players. It was a Titanic game on Thursday night and
it's such a short a turnaround but the players performed
fantastically well. Even if we had a free week, that was still
a brilliant performance. It's been a brilliant week. We've
scored 10 goals in the league and had a fantastic win over
Lazio. Mentally and physically, that game against Lazio

was draining for them but they recovered brilliantly with an outstanding performance.

We had control of the game against a very good Aberdeen side and we were magnificent. We came in at 4-0 and I couldn't ask any more really. I felt we could have had a few more in the second half with the control we had of the game. It's up there with the best 45 minutes I've seen from the players. They were relentless and the quality of their play was fantastic. I'm grateful for the win because it's a big ask to come here after Thursday and perform like they did.

We started the game well, which is important, with a brilliant individual goal from Odsonne. You can see the confidence and class from him and a lot of the other players. There were so many brilliant individual performances today. It's a great place we're in at the minute but we're not getting carried away. It's the end of a fantastic week for the players.

The mentality of the team was brilliant and their fitness levels were shining through. I have immense pride in that performance and the players can take an enormous amount of pride in their performance.

On Jeremie Frimpong's performance and first goal for Celtic

Jeremie has made a great start to his career and we are hoping that continues. He has so much energy and enthusiasm, and quality. He's probably progressed quicker than we thought so we're happy with his start here. The entire dressing room is grounded and focused, and young players like Frimpong will see that. We're all just keeping our feet on the ground and enjoying what we're doing. There could be a bump around the corner, so we always need to focus on staying on top of our game.

On the psychological importance of the Pittodrie victory

A win and a performance like that will give the players confidence going forward. It should put to bed any lingering doubts that there might be fatigue or that we need to rotate the squad a lot. When players are playing well they want to play and they've gone out and proved that on Sunday.

We're not getting ahead of ourselves but we're on a good bit of form at the minute. We knew the sense of occasion and how difficult this game would be. In terms of the character, when you have players like Brown and McGregor in the team, it drives everyone on and makes my job a lot easier.

There's been amazing consistency and level of performance from the players. The attacking intent, quality of football and fitness levels have all been phenomenal as well. Our levels are very high at the minute and we feel we can compete with a lot of teams at a lot of levels. That's where we want to be and it's about trying to maintain that consistency going forward.

v St Mirren
Wednesday, October 30th, 7.45pm

'WE WANT TO CONTINUE OUR GOOD RUN GOING AND TAKE ALL THREE POINTS'

Premiership

GOOD evening and welcome to Celtic Park for tonight's Premiership match against St Mirren. The games are coming thick and fast, with this being our third fixture in less than a week, but we have prepared well over the past couple of days and will be ready for the challenges ahead.

Last week saw another memorable European night here at Celtic Park, as we took on and beat a very strong Lazio side.

The atmosphere in the stadium was incredible, and the players produced a performance full of character, determination and no shortage of quality to take all three points against a top side. The fact that we had to come from behind to do so speaks volumes for this group of players, and I know it was a night that everyone connected with the club enjoyed.

We followed that up with the toughest of domestic tests – an away game against Aberdeen on Sunday. Pittodrie is always a difficult place to go to, especially when we had so little time to prepare, yet, again, the players responded magnificently to win 4-0.

Our performance at the weekend, particularly in those opening 45 minutes, was just brilliant and I was very proud of the players. It's up there with the best performances I've seen from the players, which is great credit to them given our recent showings against Ross County and Lazio.

We started the game well, we were relentless in our play and the quality of the football was fantastic, so I was delighted with the performance and the result.

Now we face another test tonight in the shape of Jim Goodwin's St Mirren side. Jim has his team very well-organised, and when you look at their results, it shows they are a very difficult team to score against, never mind defeat.

We want to continue our good run going and take all three points from this match. That is our intention, and with your backing, hopefully we can deliver a successful evening. Enjoy the game.

Celtic 2, St Mirren 0

Goals: Elyounoussi (49), Forrest (53).

Line-up: Forster; Bauer, Jullien, Ajer, Taylor (Hayes 88); Brown (Ntcham 69), McGregor, Christie, Elyounoussi, Forrest; Edouard (Morgan 83). Subs not used: Gordon, Elhamed, Bitton, Rogic.

NEIL Lennon was delighted with his team's performance in their 2-0 win over St Mirren and praised his players for overcoming the psychological test they have endured with the recent schedule.

On the importance of the win
It was a difficult game, difficult opponents and difficult circumstances off the back of the intensity of the last few games, and they're sometimes psychologically difficult

games. You could see that in the first half a little bit. We were a little bit hesitant, if you want to call it that.

We still created some decent chances but the response after half-time was fantastic and my only gripe is that we didn't win the game by more. We had good chances in the second half to go three or four up. It's a very good performance in the midst of a very heavy schedule of games.

On James Forrest's new deal for Celtic

James was brilliant. I don't care how much money we pay him, he's priceless to me. His all-round game tonight was exceptionally high. His inventiveness and his intelligence was excellent.

He's in his peak years now. He's scored a lot of goals already and we're only a quarter of the way through the season, which is an amazing return for any calibre of player.

He's a treble player of the year and an international player of the year. He's not going anywhere. We have him secured and he's happy.

Post-match notes

It was Neil Lennon who gave James Forrest his Celtic debut, on Saturday, May 1st, 2010. Forrest came on as a substitute for Aiden McGeady and scored in a 4-0 win over Motherwell.

NOV

2019

Neil Lennon likes November 7th. In 2012, his Celtic side defeated Barcelona on that date. In 2019, his Celtic side beat Lazio 2-1 to record the club's first ever victory in Italy.

2nd: v Hibernian (LC) N
7th: v Lazio (UEL) A
10th: v Motherwell (SPFL) H
23rd: v Livingston (SPFL) H
28th: v Rennes (UEL) H

League Cup semi-final,
Saturday, November 2, 2019
Hampden, Glasgow

Celtic 5, Hibernian 2

Goals: Elyounoussi (18, 44), McGregor (20), Brown (56, 89).

Line-up: Forster; Frimpong, Jullien, Ajer, Bolingoli (Hayes 45); Brown, Rogic (Christie 79), McGregor, Forrest (Elhamed 66), Elyounoussi; Edouard. Subs not used: Gordon, Bitton , Ntcham, Johnston.

Neil Lennon's Celtic side booked their place in the League Cup final with an impressive 5-2 victory over Hibernian at Hampden.

Speaking to the *Celtic View*, the manager expressed his delight at the performance, which continued an incredible run of consecutive domestic cup-tie wins.

On a brilliant Hampden victory

We were absolutely scintillating, I can't speak highly enough of the level of performance and mentality of the team. We were breathtaking from start to finish with our attacking intent and the chances we created. We scored five goals, which is fantastic for a semi-final, and we could have had more. We hit the post twice, their goalkeeper's made some great saves, and we've shaved things across the box. It could have been a tough game for us but the players went about their business today and made it very comfortable.

On the run of consecutive domestic cup wins

I don't know where it ranks in British football in terms of records, but it's amazing, because anything can happen on any given day. You can have a bad day, and I've had them as a player and as a manager, but Brendan put this mentality in place and we're trying to carry it on. The players just don't want to give it up, everyone's coming for them but they'll face them toe-to-toe and keep going. People want to see this run end but their pride won't let that happen. One day it will go but they are relentless in their pursuit of trophies. Not only that, but the style of football they're playing just now is fantastic.

On his trio of top Scottish talent

Those three players (Brown, McGregor and Forrest) are pretty special and they're playing some special football at the minute, allied to what's around them as well. Their consistency and willingness not to let things slide is a great barometer for the rest of them.

On two-goal hero, Mohamed Elyounoussi

He was outstanding, and that's the best he's played since he's come in. He's getting better and you can see why Southampton paid Basel a lot of money for him. Sometimes players lose their way and he's got another home, if you want to call it that, and he is thriving in the environment. He's playing with good players and we're seeing the best of him now. I think we're making him better and he's making us better. He's in a good place and he's a good kid. I really enjoyed his performance at Hampden and his football intelligence was of a very high level.

On the challenge of Celtic's next game – a tough trip to Rome

What a game to look forward to. We know what a huge incentive it is to go to Rome and get a result, and off the back of the semi-final win and the feel-good factor, psychologically, the players will all be in a good place. They'll all be wanting to play, because when you're playing well, scoring goals and playing the kind of football they are producing, you just want to keep going. You don't want to train, you just want to get out there and play again.

It's a titanic game ahead of us, we know the calibre of opposition we've got on Thursday night in Lazio, but it's not beyond us. We have had a good look at Lazio and they're a great side. The match at Celtic Park was a great game to come out the other side of, but we did have tough moments and that will be the case again on Thursday.

They've had some great wins in Serie A recently and they're a class side, but we're looking forward to it, and we know if we win or get a positive result, we can take another huge step towards qualification.

**UEFA Europa League
Matchday Four, Group E
Thursday, November 7, 2019
Stadio Olympico, Rome**

Lazio 1, Celtic 2

Goals: Forrest (38), Ntcham (90+5).

Line-up: Forster; Hayes, Ajer, Jullien, Elhamed (Bitton 81); Brown, McGregor, Forrest (Bauer 89), Christie (Nthcam 77), Elyounoussi; Edouard. Subs not used: Gordon, Taylor, Sinclair, Morgan.

Celtic's 2-1 victory over Lazio in the Stadio Olimpico was the first time that the club had won a competitive match in Italy.

It was a moment of Celtic history in the making, and Neil Lennon was full of praise for his players, and the thousands of Hoops fans in the stadium when he spoke to the *Celtic View.*

On winning in Rome – seven years to the day after beating Barca

I don't know what it is about November the seventh. The Barcelona game in 2012 was the night after the anniversary of the club's founding, so I don't know if that impacted the result. We had a special event in St Mary's Church in the Calton on the evening before the game where we spoke about the history of the club, about Brother Walfrid and how the club was formed. And on the night of the game, we just felt a crackling in the atmosphere.

Then, on the morning of the game in Rome last week, we went to the Scots College for Mass there, and, again we spoke about what Brother Walfrid brought to the club, which was built on faith, hope and love. All those little factors were, for me, synonymous with the idea that there's something brewing here.

I went to the Vatican that day, and to the Colosseum, and I saw Celtic fans sprinkled around the city, and you start to notice the wee buzz in the air. Then you walk into the stadium and you see that green and white bank behind the goal. From there, you're thinking – come on, you've got to get a taste of this, boys. You've got to want to play here.

On Olivier Ntcham's winning goal against Lazio

I knew he would score. It was a great ball from Odsonne, who was outstanding, just breathtaking at times, and he deserved a goal for his play. And I just fancied Ollie. I knew he'd dink it and we needed him because they were trying to force the issue and we just needed some fresh legs on. So not only did the starting eleven play well, but the substitutes made a huge contribution, and to win here and in the manner that we did is just spectacular.

I thought we thoroughly deserved the win and it was

just an unbelievable night for the club, an unbelievable night for the supporters who were amazing, an unbelievable night for me personally, but for the players, it's all about them. They're very, very special.

We wanted to enhance the reputation of the club in Europe. The team is doing that at the minute and you don't know where the boundaries are with this team.

We've qualified for the next round, which is fantastic, and we can maybe use the squad in some of the games coming up against Rennes and Cluj, but to have European football after Christmas is amazing.

We should really sit back and enjoy what we've seen there – the quality of our play, the bravery on the ball, the defending at times, and the goalkeeping – the sum of all parts really. What a team!

On qualifying for the knockout stages of the Europa League

It would be great to win the group and we'll try to finish with as many points as possible, but with the huge amount of games we have between now and the break it's imperative that we use the squad. It's important to give players game-time at that level so the players who haven't had a chance to play will maybe get the opportunity to play in some of these games.

The knockout round is a long way off. Come February we'll have to gauge it then, but you have the January window and hopefully we can do a bit of business and strengthen what we have already. At the minute, we're in a good place with the form, consistency and level of performance

It's not just about going deep into the Europa League, it's about winning the league and the domestic competitions we're in. If we can find that player to strengthen what we do within the budget then we'll endeavour to do that.

I don't want to get carried away because I know how difficult European football is. This current team have been really consistent away from home, particularly this season and that was always a blot against us, even in the team I played in. This team can do both.

We have maximum points in the group at home which is really important and you have to maximise the advantage you have here in Glasgow with the support we have. From my experience, it was always a great advantage going into games no matter who we played.

I've just asked for more from them on the European games. We wanted to still be dominant domestically and then make an imprint in Europe. The whole gravitas of the club changes with results like last Thursday night.

On the 10,000 Celtic fans who turned Rome green and white

I'm so happy for the fans. They were magnificent all night and even when we were a goal down, they were singing away and enjoying themselves, and you could just see them driving the team on. I said to the players, if you can build something, they will come and they have come in their thousands, and it was a great night for them.

For the first time here in my second spell, it felt like the real Celtic again. That love, pride, support from the crowd and the connection to the players in a European tie helped the team immensely. We were a goal down early and they kept the noise and tempo high and we were able to send them home happy. It was a great night for us all, and we should bottle it and hold on to it.

On the vital role of the coaching staff
I take a huge amount of pride in the performance but it's the sum of all parts. I have a great coaching staff here. They're young, dynamic and intelligent in John and Damien. Stevie Woods has been here for a while and does a great job with the goalkeepers. We're different personalities but we're all very tight and we know what we want from the group. Their work ethic is fantastic and then there are the fitness coaches and physios.

I can understand some of the fans not being too sure. There was a lot of uncertainty around me, but I have belief in myself, allied by a good support network behind the scenes, and that's manifested itself in the right way.

Neil Lennon

v Motherwell
Sunday, November 10, 3pm

'WE WANT TO KEEP OUR FINE DOMESTIC FORM UP AGAINST SOME TESTING OPPONENTS'

Premiership

WELCOME back to Celtic Park for this afternoon's game against Motherwell and it goes without saying that I hope we go into today's game on the back of a good result in Europe.

As per usual in these situations, this programme went to print before our UEFA Europa League Group E game against Lazio in Rome on Thursday evening, and, apart from the result, I also hope we have a full quota of players to choose from today with no injuries from the European trip.

That welcome also extends to Stephen Robinson and the Motherwell players and staff who have been having a great season, and that is why I hope to have a full squad to choose from today, as his side have been one of the form teams in the league campaign so far.

We go into the game this afternoon in fine domestic form ourselves, though. Since returning from the most recent international break, there were wins of 6-0 and 4-0 over Ross County and Aberdeen respectively, before our 2-0 win over St Mirren in our most recent game here at Celtic Park.

That was followed by our trip to Hampden for the League Cup semi-final against Hibernian where a 5-2 win put us into the final for the fourth consecutive season, so our domestic form is definitely something we want to keep up against very testing opponents today.

We did win our last game against Motherwell at Fir

Park with a 5-2 scoreline, but we can't read anything into that going into this afternoon's meeting as they have built up a good run of results since then and truly deserve their place well inside the top half of the table.

For us, though, it's all about what we can do on the day, and I know that our players are up for yet another challenge in the SPFL after games in the League Cup and the UEFA Europa League.

We also go into today's game on the back of some recent good news regarding the squad and its prospects as James Forrest, Callum McGregor and Scott Bain have all signed new contracts and pledged their futures to the club for the next few years.

I'm sure you're all as pleased as I am with the successful contract negotiations and we are looking forward to your backing here at Celtic Park today as you have all played your part in our results here this season. Enjoy the game.

Celtic 2, Motherwell 0

Goals: Edouard (19), Tait (og 54).

Line-up: Forster; Frimpong, Jullien, Ajer, Hayes; Brown, Ntcham, McGregor, Forrest (Christie 67), Elyounoussi (Morgan 86); Edouard. Subs not used: Gordon, Taylor, Bitton, Bauer, Rogic.

Neil Lennon's post-match reaction: 'I'm delighted with the result. It's another good performance, another clean sheet and another good win. I thought we could have won the game by more. I don't remember Motherwell having a shot on target during the game. That speaks volumes about the way the team are playing. They arrived back in Glasgow at four o'clock on Friday morning and they've gone out and performed again. I'm absolutely thrilled, and really proud of them, not just the ones who played today but the whole squad during this round of games. They've been absolutely sensational.

'Now we take stock and I think some of them need the break because it's been a really heavy load of games for everyone. The international boys will hopefully come back fit and healthy. For some of them the break will do them the world of good and we can revamp them again and get ready for the next round of games. It's good to take stock but it's not ideal. We'll have a look at things we can improve on if we can, but in the main I'm delighted by the quality and consistency of the performances. The break is frustrating because then you're coming back to a heavy load of games. It's something we need to have a look at going forward, the amount of games the big clubs play and then these guys have to play with their international teams as well, so it's a big ask.

'When we come back we'll have a couple of games this month and then we have nine games in December. It's a huge ask and then we have a break in January, which will be welcome. We can rest and recover the ones who don't go away this week and then maybe use them in the initial stages more when we go into the big block of games in December.'

v Livingston
Saturday, November 23, 3pm

'WE HAVE A GREAT GROUP OF PLAYERS HERE WHO ARE WORKING HARD FOR EACH OTHER AND THE CLUB'

Premiership

GOOD afternoon and welcome to Celtic Park for today's Premiership match against Livingston. It's good to get back to action after the international break and it's a game we're all looking forward to.

We signed off with a good home win over Motherwell, which came off the back of that fantastic night in Rome.

It was all credit to the players that, having experienced the highs of a historic European away win for the club, they remained focused at the weekend when we returned to league action and delivered a well-deserved win.

That will be our aim this afternoon as we take on Livingston, but given that Gary's team have delivered our only domestic defeat this season, we are well aware of how difficult they will be this afternoon.

That was a disappointing result for us back in October, and we are determined to ensure we don't experience that again today.

When the players return from international duty, which they have been doing throughout this week, we hope that they do so having enjoyed a successful time with their respective countries and, of course, that they have returned injury-free and ready to resume domestic action.

Today's game kicks off a busy schedule for us, with 11 games between now and the end of the year, across three different competitions.

That is what we want because it means that we are continuing to do well in these competitions, and it also means that every member of the squad will have to play their part. That's what has already happened this season, and we have a great group of players here who are working hard every day for each other and for the club.

They also need your support in all of these games and, again, our supporters have been magnificent for us throughout this campaign, home and away.

We've seen time and again how important our fans are to the team and the success we want to deliver, and this afternoon your backing can help us to enjoy another positive day at Paradise. Enjoy the game.

Celtic 4, Livingston 0

Goals: Edouard (19), Brown (57), Forrest (65, 90+3).

Line-up: Forster; Frimpong, Jullien, Ajer, Hayes (Taylor 50); Brown, McGregor, Rogic (Ntcham 75), Christie, Forrest; Edouard (Griffiths 68). Subs not used: Gordon, Bitton, Griffiths, Bauer, Morgan.

Neil Lennon spoke to the *Celtic View* after the 4-0 victory over Livingston.

On the team's display

I thought the performance at the weekend against Livingston was superb. They're a very difficult team to beat and a difficult team to play against. The win was comprehensive, as was the performance. Off the back of an international break, you always worry about momentum, but they just seemed to pick up from where they left off.

I thought we had a really good spell in the first half and then we really poured on the pressure, in terms of goals, in the second half.

The football was great and the quality of chances created was great. The pace that we played at was very good as well, so they're not far away from the expectations we have of them.

I was delighted with the performances because you just don't know how they're going to return after the time away. After five or 10 minutes I felt very comfortable in the game with the way we approached it. There didn't seem to be any rustiness and there was good tempo in our play. There was real intent and real power.

What pleased me more than anything was the goal in the 93rd minute because it showed the players weren't just content with three goals and were hungry for more. They kept piling on the pressure off the ball and kept working the opposition when they were on the ball.

On Leigh Griffiths' return to action

He needs to do extra work and stay on top of his conditioning now. He's in reasonable condition and he's working hard at that. He needs to make sure he stays fit now, because the fitter you are the more robust you become and you're less likely to pick up soft-tissue injuries like the one he had recently with the thigh strain. It's good to have him back, he adds that little bit of quality to the attacking strength that we already have.

I've spoken to him about this. I didn't come to Celtic until I was 29 and I feel like I've been here all my life. If you look after yourself and keep yourself in good condition then you can play for a long time. He certainly has the appetite for it. There's a hunger there that he has to get back playing. Hopefully, step by step, he'll get fitter and stronger with this run of games coming up now.

He's a natural-born goalscorer and he has those instincts that if he doesn't score then he doesn't think he's playing well, which, of course, isn't the case.

For people like Leigh, goals make all the difference for them. You can see his intelligence and he was unlucky not to put away the one across the box from Jeremie Frimpong. It just didn't sit up for him and it was at the wrong angle.

He also had the shot as well, so even in the cameo role he's created two great goalscoring opportunities. Hopefully that'll give him a little bit more confidence going forward.

v Rennes
Matchday Five, Group E
Thursday, November 28, 8pm

'OUR TARGET IS KEEPING OUR 100 PER CENT HOME RECORD GOING TO STAY TOP OF THE TABLE'

UEFA Europa League

WELCOME to Celtic Park for tonight's game, and that greeting also goes out to Julien Stephan, his players and the directors, staff and supporters of Stade Rennais who are here tonight.

It seems strange that it's only November, but this is the third time we have met the French side this season, and by the time our UEFA Europa League Group E games are over, we will have played CFR Cluj on no fewer than four occasions this term.

Of course, our first meeting with Stade Rennais back in July was a pre-season friendly and that, like our first competitive game against the side, was a draw and we aim to go one better tonight in our penultimate group game before the knockout stages.

We were well worth our draw over in France and I was delighted with the performance of the players in the 1-1 game over there as it set us up for what has been a very successful and pleasing group campaign.

We have won each of our Group E games since then to keep us at the top of the table and that is where we still want to be at the end of the night, and, indeed, at the end of the group-stage matches. Our success so far in this group has seen wins over both CFR Cluj and Lazio at home, and, of course, our victory over Lazio in Rome was the club's first competitive win on Italian soil.

Our target tonight is keeping our 100 per cent home run going for the supporters as well as ourselves, and we go into the game in fine form after another good domestic performance at the weekend when we beat Livingston 4-0.

Our players have the mind-set to switch from domestic to European football and they are all determined to keep our winning runs going in all competitions. We want to keep this momentum and consistency going and, again, that's also important for the supporters as much as for the team.

We have 10 points already in this group, which is a magnificent return, and we go into tonight's match intent on adding to that tally and, with your help from the stands tonight, we know we have the motivation to do just that. Enjoy the game.

Celtic 3, Rennes 1

Goals: Morgan (21), Christie (45), Johnston (74).

Line-up: Forster, Jullien, Taylor, Brown (Bitton 76), Bauer, Morgan, Christie (Griffiths 79), Ntcham, Ajer, McGregor; Forrest (Johnston 66). Subs not used: Gordon, Sinclair, Rogic, Robertson.

Neil Lennon's side beat Rennes 3-1 at home on matchday five of the UEFA Europa League group stages, and created history in the process, because it was the first time a Celtic side had won a group in either the Europa League or Champions League.

The Celtic manager spoke to the *Celtic View* about that monumental achievement.

On beating Rennes at home

It was an enthralling game. I enjoyed the game from a tactical point of view as well as the team performance. They had some milestones to achieve. Could they go beyond ten points? Could they win the group? We answered all those questions tonight. Psychologically, it wasn't an easy game with the circumstances. We handled the mentality of the game very well.

I thought we opened them up well at times. Going forward we are playing very well. The goalkeeper made a double save which was world-class. We came off it a little bit when the game looked like it was over, which is fine, I get that. We could've won the game by more.

On winning the Europa League group

It's a landmark night for us. We've never done it before, whether that be Europa League or Champions League. That's fantastic and means we can maybe get a better draw for the last 32. What pleased me is the 100 per cent record at home and then that sends out a really strong message. We've won our home games. We are unbeaten away and domestically playing great. It was important to keep that momentum going.

They played with a lot of freedom and real swagger but they aren't taking anything for granted. There was no complacency in that performance apart from the last 15 minutes which is totally understandable.

DEC

2019

The first trophy of the season was won at Hampden, with a 1-0 victory over Rangers, ensuring Neil Lennon joined Billy McNeill as the only two men to win all three domestic trophies for Celtic as player and manager.

1st: v Ross County (SPFL) A
4th: v Hamilton Accies (SPFL) H
8th: v Rangers (LC) N
12th: v CFR Cluj (UEL) A
15th: v Hibernian (SPFL) H
18th: v Hearts (SPFL) A
21st: v Aberdeen (SPFL) H
26th: v St Mirren (SPFL) A
29th: v Rangers (SPFL) H

Scottish Premiership
Sunday, December 1, 2019
The Global Energy Stadium, Glasgow

Ross County 1, Celtic 4

Goals: Christie (12 pen, 39), Rogic (66), Johnston (72).

Line-up: Forster; Frimpong, Jullien, Ajer, Taylor; Brown, Rogic (Johnston 71), McGregor (Bitton 80), Christie, Forrest; Morgan (Griffiths 75). Subs not used: Gordon, Bauer, Robertson, Sinclair.

Neil Lennon's post-match reaction: 'It was an excellent performance. I thought we started the game really well and we could have been one or two up before we got the breakthrough. Then we came off it a bit – I'm not sure if we slipped into cruise control – and we let Ross County back into the game. After that, our response again was very good. At half-time, we wanted to get rid of the complacency and just turn on the power a little bit more. We got that in the second-half and it was a great second-half display. I've got to pay tribute to the fans. I heard a story that there was a bus that left from Stranraer at half-past four in the morning. I said to the players before the game – these guys travel a long way, and it's up to you to entertain them. They're coming to watch you because you're creating a lot of good things at the minute, they're enjoying what they're seeing, and hopefully they went home happy.'

December 2019

v Hamilton Accies
Wednesday, December 4, 7.45pm

'WE'RE PLEASED TO BE TOP OF THE TABLE AND IT'S A POSITION WE'RE DETERMINED TO MAINTAIN'

Premiership

GOOD evening and welcome to tonight's Premiership game against Hamilton Accies. It's the second of nine fixtures in a busy December schedule, and we're looking forward to the match.

We're in a good run of form at the minute, having now won our last 10 games, and that's something we're determined to continue tonight.

Off the back of our Europa League win over Rennes, we headed up to the Highlands to take on Ross County at the weekend, and the team produced an excellent performance to win 4-1 and maintain our position at the top of the table.

It's always a tough test to return to domestic duties just days after the challenges of European football, but the players again showed a tremendous attitude and focus to ensure we returned home with all three points.

Tonight we're delighted, as always, to be back home and our aim, as always, is to deliver a successful 90 minutes for our supporters.

I've spoken many times about the backing we get from our fans, and that was evident again on Sunday when so many made that long journey up to Dingwall to support the team. It's something I spoke to the players about ahead of the game, and it's something that we really do appreciate.

We face a Hamilton Accies side who made it difficult for us the last time the sides met, back in September.

Brian's team will be well-organised, competitive and just as determined to get something from this match.

We've prepared well for this game over the past couple of days and our focus has solely been on the 90 minutes ahead. As is always the case, it's only when the final whistle sounds in one match can we then turn our attentions to the next game on the horizon. It's an approach which has served us well up to now and it's one that we will continue to have.

I also want to pay tribute to the players for their performances in our Europa League campaign. To be the first Celtic team to win a European group is a great achievement, and with the most points gathered in a campaign, so we're proud of what we've done in the competition.

It gives everyone something to look forward to in 2020, and when the time comes around, our aim will be to do everything we can to be successful in that competition.

We have many demands across various tournaments, and tonight the focus is on the Premiership. We are pleased to be top of the table going into this busy period of games and it's a position we're determined to maintain, starting with three points tonight. With your backing, hopefully we can enjoy another good 90 minutes here at Celtic Park.

Celtic 2, Hamilton Accies 1

Goals: Christie (13), Brown (90+2).

Line-ups: Forster; Bauer, Bitton, Ajer, Taylor; Brown, McGregor, Ntcham (Johnston 59), Forrest (Frimpong 86), Christie, Morgan (Griffiths 67). Subs not used: Gordon, Jullien, Sinclair, Rogic.

Neil Lennon's post-match reaction: 'There's no doubt that, subconsciously, the cup final would have been playing on some of their minds coming into the game tonight. You could feel it in the atmosphere and in the stadium as well. There were times when portions of the game were flat and we looked a little bit tired, and that's mental fatigue and not physical. They equalised and all of a sudden we came to life again and got the goal from Scott.

'We deserved to win the game, no question. All the wins determine which way the title goes. This is just another one. They'll all determine it. Is it a pivotal night? Not really. We go two points clear but there's still a long way to go. We keep our noses in front. Last week it was about goal difference and this week it'll be the two-point gap.'

Post-match notes

Just 24 hours after Celtic beat Hamilton Accies thanks to Scott Brown's last-gasp, winner, Neil Lennon was announced the Ladbrokes Premiership Manager of the Month for November. It was the Irishman's second award of the season, having also won it in August.

League Cup final
Sunday, December 8, 2019
Hampden Park, Glasgow

Celtic 1, Rangers 0

Goal: Jullien (60).

Line-up: Forster; Frimpong, Jullien, Ajer, Hayes; Brown, McGregor, Forrest (Bitton 66), Christie, Elyounoussi (Johnston 46); Morgan (Edouard 58). Subs not used: Gordon, Rogic, Ntcham, Bolingoli.

Celtic took on Rangers for the first piece of domestic silverware up for grabs in the 2019/20 season. It was a tough game at Hampden, with the Hoops down to 10 men midway through the second half, but Neil Lennon's side showed resilience, character and determination to win 1-0.

The victory was the fourth in a row in the competition for Celtic, while it was the Irishman's first League Cup success as manager, as he reflected on in the *Celtic View*.

On winning the League Cup
I'm thrilled and really proud. We had to dig in today. I don't think we played well in the first-half, and we had to rely on Fraser at times to make some world-class saves. We showed great resilience and a great mentality to get the goal. Then there was a red card and we had

to dig in again. Mikey had a great chance to make it 2-0, but I'm sure Rangers will say they had some great chances in the game, which they did. It's a great sort of foundation for the rest of the season.

To get that first trophy in the trilogy of trophies that we're looking to defend is important. The league is our number one priority but, so far I'm very, very proud of these players and what they've shown me collectively as a team.

I've got a great backroom staff as well and this is a wonderful group of players. I'm very lucky to work with them, I enjoy working with them and they're coming up to all the challenges that are asked of them.

On winning 31 consecutive domestic cup ties
The character and the pride and the resilience which the players had to show was incredible. That's 31 cup-ties now undefeated, over a period of three and a bit years. It's amazing, and they've faced all challenges.

We had a stiff one on Sunday. We've had them against Aberdeen, and against Hearts last season, but they keep finding ways to win and it's fantastic football ability, fantastic athleticism, but also fantastic mental strength as well.

To come through it and to win 10 major trophies is just unbelievable, as was the character and the pride and the resilience which they had to show today. I don't know who you would compare this with, either with other teams around the world or in Scottish football, but it is incredible. It's easy to give it up or think it's not our day today, but they just won't.

On joining Billy McNeill as the only men to have won all three domestic trophies as Celtic player and manager.

I didn't want to talk about it before, but it means the world to me. The League Cup was a bit of a monkey on my back. It owed me one! So it's nice to tick that box as a manager, and now we march on. I'm in esteemed company and it's an honour to be mentioned in the same breath as someone like Billy McNeill, who is a legend. I've lost two League Cup finals as a manager so it was nice for me personally to get the win. I don't think about what I've achieved, though. It's about what we as a team can achieve for this club and I'm delighted to have played a part in bringing more success.

On the first half of the 2019/20 campaign

It's been a tremendous first half of the season. In the league, we've been tremendously consistent and have a 100 per cent record at home, which is so important. Overall, I think we've exceeded our expectations in the first half of the season. People take for granted that, domestically, we're going to be the kings, but we can't do that. Consistency-wise, the players have been magnificent, and we already have a trophy in the cabinet. Psychologically, that's a great lift for us and will be positive for the second half of the season.

The European run has been magnificent too, and the players have got a huge kick out of that so far. We've played against so many good teams and beaten them, and beaten them well. If you look at the form Lazio have been on – they beat Juventus 3-1 recently and we've beaten them twice. You can't read too much into it but it bodes well for the remainder of the season.

We showed a lot of character to come from behind and win in both of the Lazio games, especially the one in Rome. That character has been there throughout the season and it was there in the win at Ibrox. That was another big win, and I was delighted with the way we played and the character the players showed.

The volume of goals was something we looked at as an area to improve on at the beginning of the season and I'm delighted with the results from that. We're getting goals from so many players and that's helped us get the results we've wanted in games. Individually, the performances have been phenomenal too. It would be unfair to name certain individuals. The group as a whole have improved and I couldn't be more proud of what they've achieved.

On going to Dubai for a winter training camp

It's very beneficial for the squad. First of all, the players get a rest and they're going to need it at the end of the month. When we start the week of training we'll do a sort of mini pre-season and get rid of all the pains and niggles and we'll do a bit of fitness work. That will stand them in good stead going into the second half of the season.

Mentally and physically, that chance to switch off is really important and it really helps the players go on and make an impact in the second half of the season. Having that rest, coupled with a bit of warm weather at that time of the year, is fantastic and it brightens their whole outlook. That gives the players a chance to refocus and set their sights on their targets for the second half of the season.

I can't underestimate how beneficial it can be. I've experienced it as a player myself under Martin O'Neill and I felt real benefit from it. We went to Orlando and then we trained at the New York Yankees training base. Some of the pre-season trips out there were awesome and we got great support out there as well.

Having that to look forward to will be really beneficial for everyone. It sharpens the mind and gives the players the chance to play at a really high level. We can try and make inroads in Europe and keep brushing up the reputation of the club. Those games are beneficial to the team and individually for the players.

UEFA Europa League
Matchday Six, Group E
Thursday, December 12, 2019
Cluj, Romania

CFR Cluj 2, Celtic 0

Line-up: Gordon; Jullien (Ajer 45), Bitton, Griffiths, Sinclair, Bauer, Morgan (Bayo 66), Johnston (Dembele 72), Ntcham, Bolingoli, Robertson. Subs not used: Hazard, Taylor, Forrest, Savoury.

Neil Lennon's post-match reaction: 'We're disappointed to lose the game but in the main I was very pleased with what I got out of it. Some of my players needed the games and needed the 90 minutes. I thought we played very well in the first half but we were very passive at the start of the second half. I'm disappointed to concede from a set-play but, overall, we've had an amazing campaign and I'm happy to have used the squad tonight because we have so many important domestic games coming up.'

Post-match notes

Despite losing in Romania, Celtic topped UEFA Europa League Group E, with a total of 13 points from their six matches. Their reward was a last 32 tie against Danish side, FC Copenhagen, scheduled for February 2020, with the first leg away in Denmark.

v Hibernian
Sunday, December 15, 3pm

'REGARDLESS OF WHAT THEY'VE ACHIEVED, THESE PLAYERS WANT TO KEEP WORKING HARD TO DELIVER SUCCESS'

Premiership

GOOD afternoon and welcome to Celtic Park for today's Premiership game against Hibernian. It is good to be back home, and we're looking forward to the match.

We're also delighted to be playing in front of you as the League Cup winners after our success at Hampden last Sunday. That was another great occasion for everyone associated with the club, and I'm sure all of you enjoyed the celebrations after the game.

It's a victory that is worthy of much praise. We have now won the League Cup for the fourth year in a row, something that has not been done since Jock Stein's great Celtic side in the 1960s, who actually went on to win five-in-a-row.

It also represents our 10th consecutive trophy win across all three domestic tournaments, and that is an incredible achievement. To have won 31 cup-ties in a row is testament to the players here – their ability, athleticism and absolute will to win, regardless of the opposition or the circumstances.

They are a great group of players, and what is so impressive is that, regardless of what success they've already achieved, they want to keep working just as hard to deliver more success to the club and our supporters.

As always, our fans were brilliant at Hampden, and I was delighted for them too. They turn out in great numbers, home and away, and in all kinds of weather, to back the team and you could see in the celebrations at Hampden that great bond between the players and the supporters.

We're in the midst of a busy month of fixtures, and today's game is the fifth of nine matches before the end of the year. I have had to write these notes ahead of Thursday night's game against Cluj, but I hope that we will have signed off our group-stage matches with another positive result.

We've had an excellent European campaign this season and we have the last 32 of the Europa League to look forward to in 2020, with the draw taking place tomorrow. However, our focus today is on today's match and what I know will be a tough test from Hibernian. Jack's done well since taking charge, and their victory over Aberdeen last weekend was very impressive.

We know from our two previous meetings this season that they will be difficult opponents and I expect that to be the case again today. However, we go into the match full of confidence and we're determined to deliver a good result in front of our own fans. Enjoy the game.

Celtic 2, Hibernian 0

Goals: Frimpong (40), Edouard (66).

Line-up: Forster; Bitton, Jullien, Ajer; Frimpong, Brown, Bolingoli, Ntcham, McGregor; Forrest (Rogic 84), Edouard (Griffiths 68). Subs not used: Gordon, Taylor, Bayo, Bauer, Morgan.

Neil Lennon's post-match reaction: 'I was so pleased with the quality of chances we created. We didn't always take them, but from 15-20 minutes in, we were dominant. We could have racked up a bit more, but in terms of quality of overall performance, I thought we were outstanding. I thought the midfield three were outstanding, and Frimpong is one of the best kids I've seen at that age. I'm delighted with what Frimpong brings to the team – offensively and defensively. He thoroughly deserved his goal, he's an outstanding talent and just watching him makes me tired, the way he runs up and down that line. With younger players, we want to look after them, but we can't hold talent back. The big question a few months ago was - could he translate his training performance into games, and he's done that. He's playing with great players, it must be said, but he's done that.'

Post-match notes

Twenty-four hours after the victory over Hibernian, Nir Bitton extended his stay with Celtic, signing a new three-and-a-half-year deal, which will see him remain at the club until the summer of 2023. Neil Lennon, who brought the Israeli internationalist to Celtic back in 2013, was pleased, as he explained to the *Celtic View*: 'I'm delighted to get Nir's deal done. I'm a big admirer of him. He had some injury problems, he's overcome them, and since I've come in the door he's been absolutely excellent. He's always maintained that he wanted to stay, so we're really pleased that we could get this bit of really good business done.'

Scottish Premiership
Wednesday, December 18, 2019
Tynecastle, Edinburgh

Hearts 0, Celtic 2

Goals: Christie (27), Ntcham (40).

Line-up: Forster; Frimpong, Jullien, Ajer, Hayes; Brown, McGregor, Ntcham, Christie, Forrest (Bitton 83); Edouard (Griffiths 83).
Subs not used: Gordon, Taylor, Bayo, Morgan, Rogic.

Neil Lennon was pleased with his side's performance against Hearts at Tynecastle, as they took all three points with a 2-0 win.

It was at the same venue where he took charge of his first game back at the club as interim manager at the end of February 2019, but while that had needed a last-gasp Odsonne Edouard goal to win the game, this time is was more comfortable for Celtic.

And the manager told the *Celtic View* he was delighted with another win during a very busy month of fixtures.

On the victory at Tynecastle
I'm delighted, I can't ask for any more, apart from maybe putting a more emphatic scoreline. We created some great chances in the second half, and we had two great chances before half-time to go three or four up.

If it had gone three or four, we could have maybe run riot, but the intensity and quality of our play at times was outstanding – on a very difficult surface. We looked good, we got another clean sheet against a team who were very much up for the game and playing with a lot of pride. We're in a good place at the minute.

On the contribution of the squad

I was so pleased with a lot of performances tonight, but more importantly, the manner in which we approached the game. We knew Hearts would be up and at it, and they were. We saw that off, and then once the game opened up we were very good. Ntcham is playing great. His finish was sublime, Jamesy worked really hard to get into the position, and as the ball came up off the surface, Olivier controlled it beautifully, and I thought Ryan's was a great finish as well. Some of the football tonight from Olly was top-class. But, listen, they were all brilliant. I thought Callum was brilliant. I thought Broony was really disciplined after the yellow card. The midfield is functioning really well, and the front three are playing brilliantly – they have been all season. The two centre-halves were great. Frimpong is… he's Frimpong. The whole team – Forster, Hayesy, they looked strong. Now, I want us to keep getting better as we go along, and they're not letting up at the moment.

v Aberdeen
Saturday, December 21, 3pm

'IF WE PLAY AS WE KNOW WE CAN DO, WE KNOW WE CAN MAKE IT TOUGH FOR ANY SIDE WHO PLAYS AGAINST US'

Premiership

A VERY warm welcome to you all here today at Celtic Park for our last game before the big day, so I'd like to wish you all a very Merry Christmas from myself and everyone else here at Celtic Football Club.

That greeting also extends to everyone here from Aberdeen and we know that Derek's side will come here intent on taking something from the game, so we have to be wary of that and go into this game with the same attitude that we have shown in every other game over the past few months both home and away.

Thanks to another great performance on Wednesday night at Tynecastle in the 2-0 win over Hearts, we go into today's meeting at the top of the table and that's where we still intend to be at the end of the day.

It won't be easy against a side who are at the top of the chasing pack, but if we go into the game playing as we know we can do, we know we can make it tough for any side who plays against us, so that's what we aim to do this afternoon.

I was delighted with the all-round performance of the team in the midweek game in Edinburgh and, apart from maybe scoring another couple of goals, which we were very unlucky not to do, I couldn't ask for any more from the men on the pitch.

There were outstanding spells of quality and intensity in our play at Tynecastle, and we'll be looking for more of the same today against Aberdeen as well as having our game-by-game aim of keeping another clean sheet.

We will approach today's game in the same manner as we did at Tynecastle, as we know that Aberdeen will be up for this game and we will be prepared for that in what has been a very busy December schedule for us.

We've won all five of our domestic matches so far this month and today is the first of another three matches to be played before the New Year and our traditional winter break, so we are determined to keep that winning run up.

Those wins mean we are in a good place, approaching Christmas with the first trophy of the season already in the bag, and we're at the top of the league, so I'd like to thank the supporters for their part in that success as they have helped us give them back the perfect Christmas present.

So, once more, I'd like to wish you all a very Merry Christmas and we aim to deliver another win for you in time for the big day. Enjoy the game.

Celtic 2, Aberdeen 1

Goals: Jullien (7), Edouard (66).

Line-up: Forster; Frimpong, Jullien, Ajer, Bolingoli; Ntcham (Johnston 61), Brown, McGregor; Christie, Edouard (Griffiths 78), Forrest (Rogic 82). Subs not used: Gordon, Taylor, Bitton, Bayo.

Neil Lennon reflected on Celtic's form in December following the victory over Aberdeen at Celtic Park.

On the team's form in December

I think we've been absolutely tremendous. Our consistency has been excellent. Our style of play and the way the players have been approaching the games, and winning the games with a certain style of play has delighted me.

I can't criticise any facet of the game at this stage, they're playing brilliant and have got the bit between their teeth. We are 10 league wins in a row, and that's very good. The way they're playing at the minute, their mindset at this stage of the season, in a heavy December, they're giving me everything.

On the league campaign

At the end of this month, they're going to get a break. They can look forward to that, but they've got to focus on the next four or five days and not listen to the outside noise. I think the team can get better, and there's more to come from them. What we've done in Europe is spectacular and what we've done domestically so far has been almost perfect.

The amount of goals we've scored, the accumulation of the points we've accrued, and the European campaign - that's all definitely exceeded my expectations. We qualified with two games to go and won the group.

We've already won a trophy, which is brilliant. Our priority is the league and we're making really good strides in that aspect. I'm absolutely delighted and I'm really proud of how the players handle themselves on and off the field.

On festive football

We'll be in on Christmas morning, and then we'll give them the afternoon and evening with their families. It's an important time of the season – from a football and a personal point of view – but it's important they spend time with their loved ones too. Still, if you come off it at all on the pitch, you put yourself under massive pressure. As a backroom staff, we prepare for the games ahead, but we can't bring that to the players until the next game in turn is dealt with. We've got to fully focus on getting the result against St Mirren.

Post-match notes

In the Christmas Special issue of the Celtic View, midfielder Ryan Christie revealed what his favourite Celtic song is – You'll Never Walk Alone. 'Everyone will say this, but it's a classic, isn't it? It's kept for those special games, which makes it that bit more special, and the timing of when it gets played in the stadium plays into that as well. For me, watching all of the big Celtic games with my Dad growing up... You'd always turn the TV up full volume, and it was amazing.'

Neil Lennon

Scottish Premiership
Thursday, December 26, 2019
St Mirren Park, Paisley

St Mirren 1, Celtic 2

Goals: McGregor (22), Forrest (32).

Line-up: Forster; Frimpong, Jullien, Ajer, Bolingoli; Ntcham, Brown, McGregor; Christie, Edouard (Griffiths 87), Forrest (Johnston 69).
Subs not used: Gordon, Taylor, Bitton, Bauer, Rogic, Bitton.

Neil Lennon's post-match reaction: 'Today's result is a great win. We could have made it a little more comfortable for ourselves, but their goalkeeper had a fantastic second half, to be fair, and some of the chances we created and some of the football was good as well. We were a bit slow getting our shots off at times, but we also scored two great goals on the counter-attack. I thought we looked dangerous all day, but I would like us to put a more flattering scoreline on the board. However, in terms of the performance, it was good.

'I can't criticise the players, they've just won their 11th game in-a-row in the league, which is fantastic form. The form we're in, are we looking forward to Sunday? Why not? We know what's at stake on Sunday, and we know if we win how much we'll be in front. After that, the players can get a well-earned rest.'

v Rangers
Sunday, December 29, 12.30pm

'TO WORK EVERY DAY WITH THE EXCELLENT COACHING STAFF AND TALENTED PLAYERS HERE IS A REAL PRIVILEGE'

Premiership

GOOD afternoon and welcome to Celtic Park for today's match against Rangers. It's not only our last game of 2019 but also our last match of the decade, and it's one that we're all looking forward to.

It's been a busy month for us, and this is our ninth match in December. The players have been superb, given the demands at this period of the season, and the aim today is to deliver another win as we head into the new year and the winter break.

Due to the programme deadlines, I've had to write these notes ahead of our Boxing Day game at St Mirren, but I hope that we go into today's match on the back of a positive result in Paisley.

This is the third derby of the season, and like the other two matches, we know this will be a very tough game. Both sides, as always, will be giving everything to win the match, and I'm sure it will be a tremendous atmosphere here at Celtic Park.

We have enjoyed two wins in the two previous clashes with Rangers this season – a 2-0 win at Ibrox and the 1-0 victory at Hampden a few weeks ago to retain the League Cup – and we want to continue that good run with a victory here at our own stadium.

However, we know how difficult our opponents will be and we will have to be at our best in order to enjoy a successful afternoon.

As I mentioned already, this is the last game of 2019

and it has been another memorable year for the club, having won the treble for the third consecutive season and lifted the first domestic trophy of this campaign.

We've also enjoyed a very impressive Europa League campaign and have a last 32 tie with FC Copenhagen to look forward to next year.

On a personal level, it has been a very eventful and enjoyable year. Coming back to Celtic as manager has been an obvious highlight, and to work every day with the excellent coaching staff and hugely talented players here is a real privilege.

I also want to thank all of you for the backing that you have given the team throughout the year. That support is absolutely vital to what we do here and for what we want to achieve, and will continue to be so, today and into 2020.

I hope that, when it comes, you all have a Happy New Year, and hopefully we can all celebrate a positive result today. Enjoy the game.

Celtic 1, Rangers 2

Goal: Edouard (41).

Line-up: Forster; Frimpong, Jullien, Ajer, Bolingoli; Brown, McGregor, Forrest (Ntcham 68), Christie (Griffiths 80), Johnston (Bitton 68); Edouard. Subs not used: Gordon, Hayes, Bauer, Rogic.

Neil Lennon's post-match reaction: 'We didn't start well at all. We had a good spell up until half-time and then came off it again. The second goal was a poor one to lose - it was a free header. From there, we were chasing the game. We had some good chances, and we missed a penalty. We competed okay, but there was no fluidity to our game. It's not like us, to be fair, but it's a test of their character now, which is good. We need to reset. It's not time to be over-critical. We've got time to think on it before we bounce back.

'We should show more experience at times and we didn't do that today. I think the whole squad needs a rest. It's not an excuse. We weren't at our best today, but I want them to look at it and know that they need to be at their best every single time in these games. Our passing was poor. Callum McGregor was the only driving force for us today, and we need more than that. We can't cancel out a full season on one game, but we're bitterly disappointed – for us and for the Celtic supporters. Off the back of winning 11 games in a row, the lack of mentality today didn't worry me, it was the lack of competitiveness. They've got to hold on to how they're feeling at the minute and use that going forward.'

Post-match notes

Celtic ended 2019 at the top of the Scottish Premiership, with 52 points from 20 games — two points clear of their nearest rivals. The Hoops won 17 games, drew one and lost two, scoring 55 goals and conceding just 13.

JAN

2020

Neil Lennon's side used the winter training camp
in Dubai to bounce back from the derby defeat
at the end of the year, and Celtic kicked off
2020 in emphatic style.

18th: v Partick Thistle (SC) A
22nd: v Kilmarnock (SPFL) A
25th: v Ross County (SPFL) H
29th: v St Johnstone (SPFL) A

Winter Training Camp
Dubai
January 2020

With Scottish football taking a break for three weeks at the turn of the year, the Celtic players were able to get a few days' holiday before heading out to Dubai for the club's winter training camp, something that had been beneficial in previous seasons.

The team were still smarting after their derby defeat in the last game of 2019, and there was a determination in Dubai to work hard in order to return to action and show that they remained the best team in Scotland.

Neil Lennon was pleased with the attitude and application of his players, and acknowledged to the *Celtic View* that it was a beneficial time for him and his squad.

On the benefits of the winter training camp
The players had five or six days off after the last match, which is a decent break after a busy run towards the end of last year. After that, we had them training very intensely at the mid-season training camp in Dubai, in very nice weather. Once we finished the sessions in the afternoon, after they'd put the hard work in, they had the chance to relax in a nice climate. Mentally and physically that's the best of both worlds and was very good for the squad as a whole.

Over there, it was great to focus on very specific aspects

of our game, and we were also working in much bigger areas, which you don't get the chance to do during the month of December. With the busy schedule, we're forced into a cycle of preparation-matchday-recovery, so it was nice to get the players training on a bigger area.

Whether we want to do a bit of tactical work, or a bit of technical work – and the players enjoy that as well, because they've not had much of a chance to do that over the last several weeks – from a coach's perspective, it's great to get them all working together.

The social benefits of the mid-season training camp are unquestionable. Having the players sharing accommodation, working and living together 24 hours a day, is hugely beneficial for morale.

The players having time with their families was crucial, but after that, so was getting them back in and re-engaging with one another after a pretty gruelling first half of the season.

On the mood within the squad

There was a good, unified spirit over there, which we've carried back to Lennoxtown and will continue driving into the second half of the campaign. A lot of these guys have known each other a long time, and the new boys have integrated themselves very well also.

At the camp, that was magnificent. And after they'd put in the hours on the training pitch, after they'd worked hard in the challenging climate, there were plenty of social activities they used to bond off the pitch too. Overall, the camp was a really good experience for them all.

Yes, we were bitterly disappointed with the outcome of the last game before the break up. We knew the significance of that game and what it meant to the fans, but we just need to use that as extra motivation going forward into the second half of the season.

There's so much to look forward to in 2020, very much so. We now have to react, we have to show an enormous amount of pride, and the motivation to get right back on the front foot again and get back to the way we've played for the vast majority of the season so far.

On the campaign so far

I think it's been an excellent first half of the season. Year-on-year, there's been a big improvement with the number of goals we've scored and the number of points we've accumulated, we topped the group in the Europa League, and we scored our 100th goal of the season in the last game. There are a lot of positives to be drawn from the first stretch of games, but we also know there is room for improvement. We know that we can get better as the season goes on, and there's a hunger about the squad to do that.

When our next game comes around, this Saturday against Partick Thistle in the Scottish Cup, the players will be revved up and raring to go. It's the start of the defence of the cup that we won last season, and it's another part of the treble that the players are determined to defend. Partick won't be easy, by any means. They'll be looking to win on their home turf, but with the break and a few weeks training under our belts, we'll be ready to go.

During December, you don't have the luxury of time, you maybe have two days before the next game and we can't really do any work with the players in that time-frame. It's tough for the rest of the squad, beyond the matchday selection, because they're required to just keep ticking over, if they're not involved in games. Over in Dubai, there was a huge difference between what we were doing on the training pitch compared to last month. Now, we look to put our preparation into action against Partick Thistle, our first match in our defence of the Scottish Cup.

On young Celts in the squad

Scott Robertson was excellent, he's a very good young professional and a good roaming footballer. We had him out in Austria at pre-season, but I don't think he's ever trained as intensely as he did over in Dubai. With that intensity and that heat, it was a new experience for him but he coped very, very well. I'm delighted with his efforts.

Everyone looked good, to be honest, and I think the break came at a good time for them all. It has re-energised them, and there were a lot of good performances at training – some that perhaps didn't get too much game-time in the first half of the season, but were keen to impress ahead of the second. That's always a big plus for us as coaches.

Scottish Cup
Saturday, January 18, 2020
Firhill, Glasgow

Partick Thistle 1, Celtic 2

Goals: Griffiths (12), McGregor (79).

*Line-up: Forster; Frimpong, Jullien, Bitton (Simunovic 6), Taylor;
Brown, Nthcam, McGregor, Rogic (Arzani 85); Griffiths
(Klimala 80), Edouard. Subs not used: Gordon, Hayes, Bauer,
Hayes, Bolingoli.*

*Neil Lennon's post-match reaction: 'We were very good, it
was a very good start and we gave a dominant performance. I
don't think the scoreline reflected our dominance in the game. I
was really disappointed with the penalty decision at the end.
However, we played vibrantly. We changed the shape of the
team, and there was good intensity to our play. I'm delighted
for Leigh. He looked sharp, scored a good striker's goal and it'll
do him the power of good. Leigh is a great player, he's a great
goalscorer, he had a great week in Dubai and he looked sharp
in training this week. He's got more to come. He looked brighter
tonight, he was trying to play off the shoulder, and I was pleased
with his performance.'*

Scottish Premiership
Wednesday, January 22, 2020
Rugby Park, Kilmarnock

Kilmarnock 1, Celtic 3

Goals: Edouard (24), Griffiths (50), Jullien (73).

Line-up: Forster; Simunovic, Jullien, Ajer; Frimpong (Bauer 88), Hayes, Brown, Ntcham, McGregor; Griffiths (Johnston 80), Edouard (Bayo 90). Subs not used: Gordon, Taylor, Klimala, Arzani.

Celtic's first Scottish Premiership match of 2020 was a tough away game at Rugby Park against Kilmarnock, but the Hoops produced an impressive showing to take all three points.

Neil Lennon was delighted with the performance, the result and the display from his forwards in particular, as he explained to the *Celtic View*.

On winning at a difficult venue
It was an outstanding performance. I don't think I've seen us come and create as many chances as we have done in such a while on a difficult surface. We scored three great goals, we're disappointed with the one we conceded, but overall, I thought we were magnificent. The attitude of the team was very, very impressive tonight.

On his striking duo of Edouard and Griffiths

Odsonne and Leigh combining up front were really good. We haven't seen that work quite as well before as we did tonight. There was a good understanding between the two of them, especially in the second half, and we looked very dangerous. Leigh's in a good place at the minute and he's enjoying his football. He's a natural goalscorer, and that's the hardest thing to do. His fitness is getting better, he had a really good trip in Dubai, he's been training well here at home too, and he scored in both the games as well. It's great to see him back scoring goals and enjoying his football again. In terms of Patryck Klimala coming in, if Griff's been given a lift by that, then that's good news for me.

On the contribution of other players

Olivier Ntcham was magnificent, although I've given him a bit of stick as I think his shooting was nearly as bad as mine at times tonight! Mikey Johnston had a great individual chance, Callum had a chance in the first half – so we're creating good chances, and the overall balance in the team and attitude and quality of the play was superb against Kilmarnock. With formations in mind, you look at your personnel, you look at who's fit, you look at your best players and think – what way can we exploit the opposition with who we have available? I'm quite happy to be flexible.

v Ross County
Saturday, January 25, 3pm

'WITH DEMANDS ACROSS THREE COMPETITIONS, THE PLAYERS ARE RELISHING THE CHALLENGES AHEAD'

Premiership

GOOD afternoon and welcome to Celtic Park for what is our first home game of 2020. We've enjoyed a good start to the year and we want to continue that today against Ross County.

That began with a Scottish Cup win over Partick Thistle last weekend. The most important thing in these games is to ensure we're in the draw for the next round, and we did just that, but in our first game back after the winter break, we produced a good performance and were comfortable winners in the end, despite the narrow scoreline.

We followed that up with an excellent display at Rugby Park on Wednesday night. It's always a difficult venue, for a variety of reasons, but I thought we controlled the game and could have won by a bigger margin than we did.

It was great to see the two strikers both get on the scoresheet, and they combined well throughout the game. That's now two goals in two games for Leigh Griffiths, and it's great to see him back doing what he does best – scoring goals.

Now our attention turns to Ross County, and our aim is to take all three points this afternoon. However, we know that they will come here determined to take something from the game so we'll have to be at our best to ensure that doesn't happen.

I know that Steve and Stuart will have been

disappointed at their Scottish Cup result last weekend, but they bounced back during the week with a good point against Hearts.

We've returned from the winter break and are immediately into a busy schedule of games, with four fixtures this month followed by eight games in February.

With those demands across three different competitions, we'll need everyone in the squad to play their part, and I know the players are relishing the challenges ahead.

Our supporters, too, will play their part. The backing we got at Firhill and Rugby Park was brilliant, as it always is, and we'll be looking for that again today as we aim for another league win. Enjoy the game.

Celtic 3, Ross County 0

Goals: McGregor (37 pen), Edouard (65, 68).

Line-up: Forster, Bauer, Jullien, Simunovic, Hayes; Brown, Ntcham (Rogic 70), McGregor; Forrest, Griffiths (Edouard 62), Johnston (Dembele 85). Subs not used: Gordon, Taylor, Klimala, Welsh.

Neil Lennon reflected on a strong performance and result against Ross County, when he spoke with the *Celtic View*.

On an impressive home win
We had a good second half against Ross County too, and some of the lads are playing really well. We're

also scoring goals, which is obviously very pleasing for us. Set pieces and decent deliveries from wide areas is something that we're always looking at. It's an important facet of the game, and can win or lose you games. We've definitely improved in that department, and it was great to see Odsonne score with his head at the weekend. Chris Jullien scored a great goal at Rugby Park as well, and, the way we see it, we've got some players now who can attack the ball and make those count.

Odsonne is such a talismanic player for us at the moment. He came on against Ross County and had such a marvellous impact with two great goals. His freshness, his influence on the game, it was great. He's such a talent!

On the qualities of James Forrest

Jamesy even had a close header against County, but was denied by a world-class save. What pleased me there was his movement. He got into the right position, connected well and was unlucky not to add to his already very good goal tally. As long as we're creating the chances, I'm confident the goals will come.

James is looking sharper again. He missed a couple of games there with a little muscle injury, but thankfully he's through that now. He got another 90 minutes under his belt on Saturday, which will do him the world of good, and he's a top player. From here, I just hope he kicks on in the second half of the season, and continues to do what he did in the first.

On Callum McGregor being put on the spot

I was so happy with Callum. It was such an important goal, the first one always is, and he took it very well. Callum is playing absolutely superbly and so consistently at the moment.

I was delighted to see him score from the penalty spot and, of course, he got another goal against Partick Thistle the week before. He's up to eight goals for the season so far, which is a great tally for him. I'm sure he'll keep adding to that as well.

Post-match notes

It was on January 30, 2019 that Neil Lennon left his post as Hibernian head coach, a decision which ultimately paved the way for his return as Celtic manager the following month. He reflected on the past year. 'You just never know where football and life will take you. Coming back to Celtic was a great opportunity, I'm very grateful for that great opportunity, and I'm enjoying what I'm doing. I'm enjoying working with these great players, and with this great club again. You just don't know where things might end up, and I obviously want to make the best of it. I'm enjoying the results we're getting at the moment, and I know the supporters will continue to get behind the team and drive us on.'

Wednesday, January 29, 2020
McDiarmid Park, Perthshire

St Johnstone 0, Celtic 3

Goals: Ntcham (6), Forrest (20), Griffiths (27).

Line-up: Forster; Simunovic (Bauer 46), Jullien, Ajer; Brown, Forrest, Ntcham, McGregor, Taylor; Griffiths (Johnston 67), Edouard (Klimala 82). Subs not used: Gordon, Hayes, Christie, Rogic.

Neil Lennon's post-match reaction: 'I was a happy man overall but the first half was outstanding. The fluidity and the quality of the play was breathtaking at times. If we played any team tonight, it would have taken a good team to stop us. I thought the first goal was outstanding. Olivier was outstanding tonight. He's got better and better as the season's gone on. Forrest was brilliant. He's back to his very best, he scored a goal and his all-round game was superb.

'I thought Taylor was outstanding too, the best he's played since he's been here. We were working on it a little bit yesterday and he put three or four good crosses in which I hadn't seen from him before so I was very impressed with how he did tonight. You always want more goals but we had to change the shape with Jozo coming off. He's gone above and beyond the call of duty since coming back and has been playing through the pain barrier. He was in a bit of pain, there's no damage but we'll give him rest.'

FEB

2020

Celtic's domestic form continued to impress, including a tough win at Pittodrie, but there was Europa League disappointment for Neil Lennon as his side were knocked out of the competition.

2nd: v Hamilton Accies (SPFL) A
5th: v Motherwell (SPFL) A
9th: v Clyde (SC) A
12th: v Hearts (SPFL) H
16th: v Aberdeen (SPFL) A
20th: v FC Copenhagen (UEL) A
23rd: v Kilmarnock (SPFL) H
27th: v FC Copenhagen (UEL) H

Scottish Premiership
Sunday, February 2, 2020
New Douglas Park, Hamilton

Hamilton Accies 1, Celtic 4

Goals: Edouard (35, 81), Jullien (78), Forrest (90).

Line-up: Forster; Welsh (Rogic 76), Ajer, Jullien, Brown, Taylor (Hayes 75), Forrest, McGregor, Ntcham (Christie 65); Griffiths, Edouard. Subs not used: Bain, Bauer, Christie, Arzani, Klimala.

Celtic continued their impressive start to 2020 with an emphatic 4-1 victory over Hamilton Accies that took the Hoops seven points clear at the top of the Premiership table.

Speaking to the *Celtic View*, Neil Lennon was delighted with the contribution of the squad.

On his central midfielders

I know that role and so do those players, and it's not easy doing what they do. They're so intelligent. Scott Brown at 34 is playing as well as he ever has. He has such an aura and influence about him, and he reads the game brilliantly. He looks great and has always been a naturally fit athlete. His football is as good as ever and I've been delighted with what he brings to the team. Away from the pitch as well he's a great influence on a lot of the younger players. They all look up to him and respect him.

James Forrest is back to his very best as well, and Callum McGregor is a metronome. He's so consistent with his passing, his reading of the game, his play and he's got goals this season. They've all made a huge contribution this season so far. The level and standard they've set themselves means people sometimes take them for granted. It's our job just to keep them ticking over.

Ryan's energy is fantastic and his enthusiasm is fantastic, but more than anything it's his quality. The quality of the ball for the second goal was De Bruyne-esque. Having Ryan back after being out for a month is such a bonus for us. Tom Rogic came on and did a great job and Jonny Hayes had a great game, but Ryan has and is having a fantastic season and we'll see more of that as we go along.

On two-goal hero, Odsonne Edouard

He's certainly a mercurial talent. If you look at both of his goals at the weekend, he makes them look easy, but they're very difficult. His second goal against Hamilton came from a great link up with Tom Rogic. The free-kick was special because it was so close up and to get it up over the wall, and in the corner was amazing. His all-round game is improving all the time and he's a player playing with a lot of confidence. He's quiet and then all of sudden he bursts into life and you see these touches of genius and flashes of brilliance that take your breath away. His personality is just so easy-going and he's very happy with life at the minute.

He's got 22 goals already this season which is a fantastic return for him and, at times, he's had to take on the responsibility all by himself. With the change of shape, he has that bit more support around him and seems to be thriving on that. Edouard's movement off the ball is brilliant and it's helped by having another player around him like Leigh Griffiths.

On hitting a century of goals since his return to Paradise

We're always trying to be positive and attack-minded. With the back door shut and the character and resilience in the team, we're always wanting to score more goals which is always important as well. We're training them as best we can at the minute. The rest and recovery is really important with that as well. I felt in December we came off it a little bit and were scoring in twos but since we've come back we're scoring in threes and fours. Scoring goals is a nice habit to have. We have Ryan, Odsonne and Jamesy all on double figures and Callum's scoring goals too. Jullien's been contributing with some really important goals and then Leigh's been on goalscoring form just now as well, which is great. They just want to be the best they can be.

Scottish Premiership
Wednesday, February 5, 2020
Fir Park, Motherwell

Motherwell 0, Celtic 4

Goals: Edouard (9, 80), Griffiths (51), McGregor (75).

Line-up: Forster; Simunovic, Jullien, Ajer; Brown, Forrest, Ntcham (Rogic 86), McGregor, Taylor; Griffiths (Christie 70), Edouard (Klimala 84). Subs not used: Bain, Welsh, Bolingoli, Elyounoussi.

Neil Lennon's post-match reaction: 'It was a spectacular second half performance against a very good side who caused us a few problems in the first half. The quality of our play and the motivation, hunger and desire and quality of the goals was spectacular. All credit to the players, it's a magnificent win and it's not often you come here and win 4-0. Motherwell are a good side and well coached but I can't speak highly enough of my coaching staff and players. They've started the second half of the season brilliantly. I thought we played really well against St Johnstone in the first half but when you consider the opposition tonight and where we were then this was probably the best we've played since returning. The players are in a good place.

'I've played with good strikers and, at times, it's telepathic. Those two have football intelligence in abundance. Leigh Griffiths is a natural centre forward. He can get better and fitter but he has natural footballing intelligence. The two of them linking together doesn't surprise me at all. He's working hard at his game and I just hope he stays on top of things now because he's an asset for us now, there's no question of that. Odsonne's just special. When he's on that form he's a joy to watch. It was a great finish for the first goal. His link-up play with Leigh was very creative and good to watch. He's just an outstanding footballer all-round and he's so important to us at the minute.

'Against Clyde this Sunday, we'll make a few changes for sure. We don't want to overdo it, but there are a few players bubbling under. Ryan Christie could do with a game, Elyounoussi could use some time on the pitch as well, but we'll still field a strong team. At the moment, we're just concentrating on ourselves, and the motivation and incentives are strong. We're keeping calm and taking each game on its own merits.

'Danny Lennon is a football man, he's technically astute and will come with a game-plan. We'll be wary. We're not going to take it lightly. We're the cup holders and we want to defend the trophy vigorously. We've got to make sure we're focused, profession and do everything we can to get to the next round.'

Post-match notes

Callum McGregor scored his eighth goal of the season with a sublime half-volley for Celtic's fourth goal at Fir Park. He said of the goal: 'It took a wee bobble which invited me to hit it and it was one of those nights where you see it flying into the top corner. It's up there with the Scottish Cup final one against Motherwell.'

Scottish Cup
Fifth Round
Sunday, February 9, 2020
Broadwood Stadium, Clyde

Clyde 0, Celtic 3

Goals: Ntcham (16), Brown (40), Bayo (89).

Line-up: Bain; Bauer, Jullien, Ajer, Bolingoli; Brown, Ntcham, Christie; Forrest (Hayes 71), Klimala (Bayo 76), Elyounoussi (Shved 86). Subs not used: Forster, Taylor, Griffiths, Soro.

Neil Lennon's post-match reaction: 'We picked a strong team against Clyde, which was important, even though we made a few changes, but it was good for the likes of Ryan Christie and Mo Elyounoussi to get on the pitch and get a feel for the game again, because they'll be important players going forward. I was delighted with the rest of them, too, and it was a good professional performance.'

Post-match notes

Olivier Ntcham celebrated his 24th birthday on February 9 with Celtic's opening goal against Clyde. Scott Brown, who also scored, said: 'Today was all about Olly, it was his birthday and what a strike it was to start everything off.'

169

v Hearts
Wednesday, February 12, 7.45pm

'I'M ABSOLUTELY DELIGHTED WITH THE START THAT WE'VE MADE TO 2020 AND THE FORM THAT WE'RE IN'

Premiership

GOOD evening and welcome to Celtic Park for tonight's match against Hearts. After four consecutive away games, it's good to be back home, and we're all looking forward to this game.

We've enjoyed a great start to 2020, both in the league and also the Scottish Cup, and that continued at the weekend with our victory over Clyde.

We've hit the ground running since coming back after the winter break, although we know that there's still a long way to go in the campaign, so we're not getting carried away. But I'm absolutely delighted with the start that we've made to 2020 and the form that we're in.

February is a busy month for us, with eight games between now and the end of the month, and we've got another big game coming up tonight against Hearts.

They're finding their feet under the new manager and Daniel has brought some new players in, so it'll probably take a bit of time to adapt, but they can be dangerous opponents because they've got a bit of quality with the likes of Liam Boyce, Steven Naismith and Conor Washington.

It's important for us to keep our run going, and it was good to give the likes of Ryan Christie and Mohamed Elyounoussi some valuable game-time at the weekend, while also enabling others like Callum McGregor and Odsonne Edouard to have a rest.

We've also got some of the other injured players

returning to training, which is a great boost, and they'll all be needed in the weeks and months ahead as we continue to complete across several fronts.

Like all of you, I was shocked to hear the news about Jackie McNamara, and my thoughts and prayers, along with everyone at the club, are with Jackie and his family at this time. A great Celtic player, a brilliant team-mate and a good friend, Jackie has always been much-loved by his fellow Celtic supporters, and I know the whole Celtic Family are sending their best wishes to him.

Celtic 5, Hearts 0

Goals: Ntcham (30), Jullien (46), McGregor (53), Christie (66), Simunovic (80).

Line-up: Forster; Simunovic, Jullien, Ajer, Forrest (Elyounoussi 71), Taylor; Brown, Ntcham (Rogic 78), McGregor; Griffiths (Christie 64), Edouard. Subs not used: Bain, Bauer, Hayes, Bayo.

Neil Lennon's post-match reaction: 'The players were magnificent tonight. Their desire and hunger to play, score goals and run had everything you want as a manager from a team and I got that tonight. It was an emphatic victory and an outstanding second-half performances. To score five goals and your strikers not to score shows a great team effort. We changed the shape a little in the second half and got more reward with that. We scored from set-pieces as well, which was very pleasing. There's a long way to go and there'll be twist and turns along the way so we just need to focus on each game as it comes along.'

Scottish Premiership
Sunday, February 16, 2020
Pittodrie, Aberdeen

Aberdeen 1, Celtic 2

Goals: McGregor (10), Ajer (82).

Line-up: Forster; Bitton, Jullien, Ajer; Taylor (Hayes 24), Brown, Forrest, McGregor, Ntcham (Rogic 79); Griffiths (Christie 58), Edouard. Subs not used: Bain, Frimpong, Elyounoussi, Bayo.

A trip to Pittodrie is always a tough test, and difficult weather conditions only made it even harder for the Hoops.

But Neil Lennon, talking to the *Celtic View*, identified the determination within his squad as key to taking all three points against Aberdeen.

On a battling performance at Pittodrie

I'm thrilled. It's a massive win in treacherously difficult conditions to play football. All credit goes to the players. They dug out a massive result for us. You can't always play quick, slick football and they had to grind it out today.

It's a good sign to get the result. It shows character and resilience, and that they're a team. There's good solidarity within them and they keep going. The fitness levels are great as well but we're not getting ahead of ourselves because there's still a lot of football to be played. In the context of the run that we're on, it's a big win.

We didn't want to drop points but it was looking like it, and a point at Pittodrie sometimes can be a decent result. In these conditions the game could have gone either way but we came up with a really important piece of football. A point away from home isn't the worst result in the world but we're always trying to think of getting a goal. The subs we brought on were forward-thinking players and the ones who could create something.

On changing the shape of the team
The tactical changes worked quite well for us and we started creating good opportunities. Jonny had a great chance. Then we scored and then Odsonne had a great chance. The change helped the players, there's no question of that. Jamesy opened the pitch right up and the pass was perfectly weighted. Kris showed a lot of composure to finish it off. It was a great goal and an important goal.

James is a fantastic player who's back to his very best, and bang at it. His play for the second goal at Aberdeen, the way he opened the pitch up and passed for Kris was perfect. He's a great finisher once he's in there as well. I'm absolutely delighted with Jamesy at the moment, and I wouldn't bet against him upping his numbers even more between now and the end of the season.

On Kris Ajer's winning goal

It's the composure of Kris' goal that's so impressive. He had time, and sometimes that can be a disadvantage, but he's taken a good touch, he had a look where the goalie is, and he finished it with aplomb. Would I have been proud of that? 'Yes!' But I probably wouldn't have got that far up the pitch. Kris' run was incredible, as was his desire to get there. He's ate up 60, maybe 70 yards to get into that position. He's got a great will to win, he's fantastic in that aspect, and he's having a fantastic season again.

On the backing of the Celtic supporters

I appreciate the fans making a long trek in horrible conditions. I appreciate everything they bring us and I thought they were magnificent. Even at 1-1, when the game could have gone either way, they were still making a lot of noise.

And I'm delighted with the players, I'm delighted with their attitude and their will to win, and I'm delighted with their fitness levels. It's never easy up there, and at that time of day. There's a low sun, there was a strong wind, and it wasn't conducive to playing the sort of football we're accustomed to.

To win in that manner was fantastic for us, and can give us a real boost going into Thursday, and then again on Sunday against Kilmarnock at Celtic Park.

UEFA Europa League
Round of 32, first leg
Telia Parken Stadium, Copenhagen
Thursday, February 20, 2020

FC Copenhagen 1, Celtic 1

Goal: Edouard (14).

*Line-up: Forster, Frimpong (Simunovic 84), Jullien, Ajer, Hayes;
Brown (Bitton 73), Ntcham (Elyounoussi 60), McGregor; Christie,
Edouard, Forrest. Subs not used: Bain, Bayo, Rogic, Bolingoli.*

Neil Lennon's post-match reaction: 'It was a brilliant start and
we could have been two or three up in the first half. We had
really good control of the game and Fraser only really had one
effort to deal with. It was a brilliant move for the goal, nice and
slick from Ryan Christie and Callum McGregor, who I thought
was brilliant again tonight. It was a beautifully-weighted pass
into Odsonne's feet and it was a class finish from a class player.

'I thought Odsonne might have done that with the first one and
lifted that chance over the keeper. On the counter-attack I thought
we had some great chances to put the tie beyond Copenhagen but
we weren't ruthless enough tonight and in the end we had to rely
on Fraser to make the save from the penalty. I'm delighted that
we have an away goal to take back to Celtic Park next week. If
we can play like we did in the first half we should be okay.'

v Kilmarnock
Sunday, February 23, 3pm

'WE'VE ESTABLISHED A LEAD AT THE TOP OF THE TABLE BUT WE'LL CONTINUE TO TAKE EACH GAME AS IT COMES'

Premiership

GOOD afternoon and welcome to Celtic Park for today's Premiership match against Kilmarnock. It's our seventh match in what has been a very busy month of fixtures, but it's one that we're looking forward to, particularly since we're playing at home.

We come into this game on the back of the first leg of our Europa League tie against FC Copenhagen, and due to the programme deadlines, I've had to write these notes ahead of Thursday night's game.

It goes without saying that I hope we're going into today's game on the back of a positive result in Denmark and one that sets us up for the return leg here at Celtic Park this coming Thursday.

For now, though, our focus is solely on the 90 minutes ahead and the challenges that Kilmarnock will pose for us.

We go into this match full of confidence after a strong start to 2020, which included a win over today's opponents at Rugby Park.

That match, like all our encounters with Kilmarnock, was a tough one and we're expecting that to be the case again this afternoon.

Alex has got his team playing very well, and up until last weekend's result against Hibernian, they had been enjoying a very impressive run of results in February, which included a home win over Rangers and a draw at Pittodrie.

And we know from our own experience of playing away to Aberdeen last weekend just how difficult a venue that is to get anything from.

So we are anticipating a tough 90 minutes ahead, and we know we'll have to be at our best if we want to take all three points.

We've established a lead at the top of the table and that's something we want to maintain. We know that there's still a lot of football to be played between now and the end of the season, and so we will continue with our approach of focusing on each game as we go into it.

It's an approach which has served us well up to now, and we hope will continue to do so in the future.

I also want to thank all our supporters for their incredible support of the team, both home and away. I've already mentioned the heavy fixture schedule which, for the players, is very demanding.

That is the case for our fans, too, but they turn up to every game in great numbers to give the team the fantastic backing that means so much to all of us, and which plays a crucial part in any success we're able to deliver.

I know that backing will be vital again today. Enjoy the game.

Celtic 3, Kilmarnock 1

Goals: Ajer (29), Edouard (33), Griffiths (62).

Line-up: Forster; Simunovic, Jullien, Ajer; McGregor, Frimpong, Rogic (Elyounoussi 74), Christie, Taylor; Griffiths (Bitton 82), Edouard (Bayo 74). Subs not used: Bain, Bayo, Klimala, Bauer, Bolingoli, Elyounoussi

Neil Lennon's post-match reaction: 'The performance and reaction to going a goal down pleased me most. Our reaction was excellent and we all know how difficult a team Kilmarnock can be to break down. We did that very well and in the second half we were outstanding. It was a brilliant performance and a really good day for us. You need patience at times. They block the centre off, they have experienced players who do that very well and they have good strikers who are a handful. We had to be mindful of that when we were attacking and our concentration at the back had to be good.

'In the second half, our players came out and were simply irresistible at times. I can see Callum taking on the role of captain, but in that position in midfield? Maybe when he's the other side of 30! He has a lot to offer higher up the pitch. You can see how good a player he is and that's an understatement. At this level he's a different class. He'd certainly be a contender for Player of the Year with the way he's playing. I thought his performance today was immaculate.'

v FC Copenhagen
Round of 32, second leg
Thursday, February, 27, 8pm

'EUROPEAN NIGHTS HERE AT CELTIC ARE RENOWNED AND WE WANT TO MAKE TONIGHT ANOTHER SPECIAL OCCASION'

UEFA Europa League

GOOD evening and welcome to Celtic Park for tonight's UEFA Europa League match against FC Copenhagen. I would also like to extend that welcome to our visitors from Denmark. We received a great welcome in Copenhagen last week – players, management and supporters – and we hope that they are similarly welcomed here.

It was, as expected, a tough game against a very good opponent, and we know that will be the case again tonight, particularly with the tie finely balanced after the 1-1 draw last Thursday night.

We were pleased to score an away goal, which is always the aim in these situations although, given how well we played, particularly in the first half, we could well have scored a few more goals.

However, FC Copenhagen also showed the attacking threat they possess, scoring a goal and having the chance of a second goal when they were awarded a penalty. But Fraser Forster once again proved his worth with a great spot-kick save.

It was, of course, our first competitive game with the VAR system in operation, and that will be the case again tonight here at Celtic Park. And even though it has often provided talking points in games elsewhere, it's not something we're thinking about or focused on.

Our preparations since Sunday's good win over Kilmarnock have been solely on how we play against

FC Copenhagen with a view to progressing to the last 16 of the competition, and I know that has also been the case with Stale Solbakken and his staff ahead of this match.

European nights here at Celtic Park are renowned in football, and we want to make tonight's match another special occasion. I thought the crowd was tremendous on Sunday, and you could hear the way they roared on the team after we went a goal down.

Our fans definitely played their part in that win, and they can play their part again tonight as we look to get a positive result that will take us into the last 16 of the competition. Enjoy the game.

Celtic 1, FC Copenhagen 3

Goals: Edouard (83 pen).

Line-up: Forster, Ajer, Jullien, Simunovic, Taylor, Brown, McGregor, Forrest, Rogic, Elyounoussi (Griffiths 70), Edouard. Subs not used: Bain, Bitton, Bayo, Hayes, Bolingoli, Frimpong.

Neil Lennon's post-match reaction: 'As you can imagine I'm hugely disappointed. In the first half, we were in total control, they had a couple of corners, but we had all the flow, we hit the post and we played balls across the goal. We then made a mistake which gave them oxygen. We had to change the shape to get back into the game. We did that and then we equalised, deservedly so. But we mismanaged the game and shot ourselves in the foot for the second goal, and then the other after that.'

MAR

2020

With a 13-point lead at the top of the table following an emphatic win over St Mirren, and with just eight games to go, Neil Lennon's side were heading inexorably towards the title. Then everything came to a sudden and unexpected halt.

1st: v St Johnstone (SC) A
4th: v Livingston (SPFL) A
7th: v St Mirren (SPFL) H

Scottish Cup quarter-final
Sunday, March 1, 2020
McDiarmid Park, Perth

St Johnstone 0, Celtic 1

Goal: Christie (81).

Line-up: Forster; Bitton, Jullien, Ajer; Brown, Forrest, Christie,
McGregor, Taylor (Hayes 76); Griffiths (Rogic 65), Edouard
(Bayo 86). Subs not used: Bain, Klimala, Frimpong, Elhamed

Celtic continued their remarkable run of wins in domestic
cup ties to 34 with a narrow victory over St Johnstone. The
victory put the Scottish Cup holders into the semi-final of
the competition.

And Neil Lennon, speaking to the *Celtic View*, praised his
players' application and attitude for their continuing cup
success.

On the ongoing run of domestic cup-tie victories
It's remarkable. It's something the players are really proud
of, and I would love them to get to 36 – because that then
means that we've won the Scottish Cup again. The next
one is Aberdeen in the semi-final, and that's not going to
be easy, but the team are doing really well.

It was a difficult game against St Johnstone on a difficult

pitch in difficult conditions. I thought we could have won by more, but all told, it was comfortable, and we were in control.

I was delighted to come through a sticky quarter-final in a game that I felt flattered the home side. We really could have been two or three goals better off, but it was a great win and now we have a really difficult semi-final that we're all looking forward to.

On the win over St Johnstone at McDiarmid Park

We went into Sunday's game and it was freezing, it was windy, the pitch was a bog, and the importance of the result was so, so important. Off the back of any defeat, the last thing you want is another one, but off the back of a European defeat, there's that extra incentive to bounce back in domestic football. To do that, concentration levels need to be as high as they possibly can be.

I thought we thoroughly deserved to win the St Johnstone game. The mentality of the team is fantastic, I don't know how they keep doing it, but it's wonderful. That said, though, it just takes one mistake, one moment, one off-day, which is why we take nothing for granted.

We're in a really good position in the league, we're in the semi-final of the Scottish Cup, and we've got the League Cup won already – so there are a lot of positives to be drawn over the last few days, even though we were bitterly disappointed to exit Europe.

They've bounced back really well and we've still got a

lot to play for. I think the boys can get better and I've said that to them. I think we push on and finish the season as strongly as we possibly can. I think there's more to come from this team and squad, and there's no room for complacency.

On the winning goal

I still don't know who scored! Chris Jullien made the run, and I think he made the goal, but it was a great delivery in. If Ryan takes it, that's great, that's his 19th at club level for the season so far, so he's having a tremendous campaign. From a midfielder as well, that's an incredible return.

Jamesy is on 16 as well, and Odsonne is on 27, which means we're getting a lot of goals from quality players. As long as we continue to create the quality of chances we have been, then that's the most important thing for me.

On the prospect of a semi-final clash with Aberdeen

We had a great win against Aberdeen this time last year in the same round, but anything can happen on any given day. It's really important that we're in this year's semi-final, and we're all looking forward to it and the challenge it poses. We've played well at Hampden in recent years, which is why this team's record is so impressive, but we take nothing for granted. We'll park the Scottish Cup in our minds for now, focus on the league, and then prepare ourselves for Aberdeen when the time comes.

Scottish Premiership
Wednesday, March 4, 2020
Tony Macaroni Arena, Livingston

Livingston 2, Celtic 2

Goals: McGregor (16), Rogic (90+2).

Line-up: Forster, Bitton, Jullien, Ajer, Brown, Forrest, Christie (Griffiths 76), McGregor, Taylor (Frimpong 62), Edouard, Elyounoussi (Rogic 68). Subs not used: Gordon, Bayo, Hayes, Elhamed.

Having lost to Livingston at the Tony Macaroni Stadium earlier in the season, Celtic knew it would a tough test on their return, and so it proved.

The Hoops dominated for much of the game but, in the end, needed a late Tom Rogic equaliser for a share of the points, and the manager reflected on the game in the *Celtic View*.

On the performance
I'm delighted with the performance and I thought we thoroughly deserved the three points. The way we played pleased me more than anything. The performance was brilliant, so that's why I'm disappointed we haven't won the game. We were relentless and some of our passing and willingness to get the ball back was brilliant.

Callum McGregor got us off to a great start and

Edouard hit the post. We had a great chance in the second half. Livingston were hanging on and hanging on but in the end we broke them.

We got the least we deserved. I had total belief that we would get the equaliser and then Tom came up with the goods.

The team were fantastic and their mindset, their intensity and the will to win was all there. Against a difficult opponent, on a difficult pitch, we were absolutely outstanding.

On drawing the match

I'm disappointed to lose the first points of 2020 and I didn't think we deserved it because we dominated the game for long periods. We can't give away sloppy goals against any opposition because I don't want us to be chasing games. We set standards and the standards are set high. These are the first points we've dropped which is bitterly disappointing but in the context of the evening it's okay.

On Celtic's late goal hero

Tom's been great. In recent weeks he's been outstanding. Astroturf pitches aren't great for him but we knew at some stage we'd need him. We got a good 25 minutes out of him and he came on to give us an important goal.

v St Mirren
Saturday, March 7, 3pm

'WE'LL HAVE TO BE BANG AT IT, BUT IF WE CAN OPEN THEM OUT, I HOPE IT'LL BE A GAME TO LOOK FORWARD TO'

Premiership

GOOD afternoon and welcome to Celtic Park for today's Premiership match against St Mirren. As always, it's good to be back home and it's a game that we're all looking forward to.

The match comes at the end of another busy week which presented us with a number of different challenges.

Last weekend, we took on St Johnstone in what was a difficult Scottish Cup tie at McDiarmid Park. We battled tough opponents, as well as the elements and a tricky playing surface, to secure a good victory and a place in the semi-final of the competition.

We followed that up with another tough game, this time in the league, and at a venue that has proven difficult for us in the past couple of seasons.

We had to settle for a point against Livingston, and although it was disappointing that it ended our 100 per cent domestic record in 2020, it showed the character and determination of this group of players.

I thought we were excellent on the night, and deserved more than the point but we're still pleased that, ahead of today's match, we extended our lead at the top of the table.

We face a St Mirren side who have proved difficult already this season in both of our previous meetings. Jim Goodwin has done a brilliant job there, and he's made St Mirren far more resilient than they were.

It's a game in which we'll have to be bang at it. We can't take any chances, but again, if we can open them out, then I hope it'll be a game to look forward to.

I was also delighted to join Doddie Weir at Celtic Park earlier in the week for the launch of Celtic FC Foundation's Lions' Road Charity Match, which will take place here on Friday, May 8.

Doddie is an inspirational figure, and is doing so much to raise awareness about Motor Neurone Disease which, sadly, he is now battling.

This match will raise vital funds to help research into the disease, and I'm sure that Celtic supporters, as well as sports fans in general, will come along on the night to support this and enjoy a great occasion.

Celtic 5, St Mirren 0

Goals: (Griffiths (18, 44, 74), Edouard (55), McGregor (89 pen).

Line-up: Forster, Bitton, Jullien, Ajer (Elhamed 80), Forrest, Brown, Taylor, McGregor, Rogic (Christie 72), Griffiths, Edouard (Elyounoussi 76). Subs not used: Gordon, Frimpong, Hayes, Bayo.

Neil Lennon was delighted with the 5-0 home win over St Mirren, with Leigh Griffiths netting a hat-trick.

When he spoke to the *Celtic View*, the Hoops boss was looking ahead to the weekend derby at Ibrox, and not anticipating that the St Mirren game would effectively turn out to be the last game of the 2019/20 season.

On the 5-0 victory over St Mirren

It was an emphatic win and a clean sheet off the back of a hard game on Wednesday. It could have been a tricky one but we dealt with it well. There was a good work ethic from us on and off the ball and I couldn't have asked any more of the side.

We're scoring a good volume of goals and a lot of it comes through Edouard and Griffiths. They're both bona fide centre-forwards and Odsonne's goal ratio this season has been terrific. I'm pleased for him getting his goal as well and we could have had a few more.

On Celtic's hat-trick hero

I'm delighted for Leigh, and he looked more like his old self. The third goal summed up Leigh Griffiths – a quick turn and he smashes it into the corner. We've not seen that from him in a while. The second goal was brilliantly worked and the first goal gave him a lot of confidence so he can be really happy with his day's work. Leigh's getting there. There's more to come from him and he'd tell you that himself. There are definitely good signs. He can get fitter, stronger and add more endurance into his game if he wants to play longer at this high level.

I'm so pleased for him because he's come a long way and that hat-trick will mean a lot to him personally. It'll give him a huge lift. Now he knows he can still do it and we all knew he could. He's answered all his critics. People were saying he was finished here, but that was never the case with him. My backroom team worked with him and the fitness coaches worked with him so he owes the club a lot, and with performances like that he's starting to repay it.

On looking ahead to the Glasgow derby

We have a full week to prepare for this, so we'll go into it strong and try to win the game using the style of football that's conducive to the way the fans want us to play and what the club's used to.

Having a week to get ready for the game is a novelty. It's been non-stop for us. The break was good and then January and February were heavy months, but we got a lot of work into them in Dubai and accomplished a lot of good things, so it's important we maintain our consistency now and don't take our eye off things.

We've lost some important players at key times in the season. We've even changed the system at times and adapted to that and I think in the main now we have almost a full complement. Mikey Johnston's the one real long-term injury but the rest of the squad seem pretty healthy up until now. The volume of games is bound to take its toll but the players have been absolutely fantastic since the turn of the year.

The extra couple of days working with the players does us good as well. It gives us more time to think about things and lighten the load a bit for the players.

LOCK
DOWN

2020

The end of the 2019/20 campaign was unexpected
and unprecedented, with the football season
postponed due to the COVID-19 coronavirus
pandemic.

Celtic's 5-0 victory over St Mirren on March 7 had seen Neil Lennon's side go 13 points clear at the top of the Premiership table with just eight matches remaining. The first of those eight games was scheduled for Sunday, March 15 at Ibrox, with the Hoops determined to record their second win at the stadium that season to further cement their position as league leaders.

On Friday, March 13, however, the SPFL announced that the weekend calendar of fixtures, and those of the following midweek were postponed in the interests of the health and safety of players, match officials, staff, supporters and the general public. It would subsequently transpire that there would be no resumption of the 2019/20 season.

With the country effectively moving into lockdown, Neil Lennon and his players had to train individually and remotely while they awaited further news of what was to happen with the remainder of the season.

And for the *Celtic View*, that meant utilising Zoom, Skype and FaceTime to maintain contact and speak to the manager.

On the March 13 decision to postpone football fixtures in Scotland

I'm not a health expert, the decision to postpone the league has come from people far more well-qualified than me. The public health is the most important thing. If that decision has been taken, then we back it. No players or staff have displayed symptoms. It's been business as usual. We were training today and then we got word that the Rangers game was cancelled. We've given the players a few days off until we can sit down on Monday and see where we go from here. Hopefully, come Monday, we'll have a better idea of what's ahead of us.

It's unprecedented, I've never experienced anything like this in my career, and I'm sure everyone is in the same boat. The gym is here for the players if they want to use it, and we'll try to get back to business as usual. We were preparing for Sunday's game, but we understand, while still disappointed. To finish the league as is stands would be the ideal scenario. From what I gather, this is going to get worse before it gets better but we don't know what's going to happen, to tell you the truth.

This virus has taken people. It's taken loved ones. We've got players from all around the world, and these players are our priority and have been since this outbreak. We've tried to insulate and protect them, and obviously the people that work here as well. It's so unfortunate. It's a nightmare situation. We have to put everything sporting aside. Your health is your wealth, at the end of the day.

If the season was scrapped we'd be the champions, and rightly so, because we're 13 points clear. In most of the other leagues, I'd say it's the same. Dundee United would need to be promoted as well. If you're talking about the armageddon of the league being cancelled or stopped, then it should go on the average points total, which would make us champions and rightly so.

Ideally, you'd like to get the fans back in. I've watched a few games this week behind closed doors and it's not great. You want your fans in there to back you because they play such a big part. The most important people in football are the players and the supporters. You can't have one without the other, really. I'm not a big lover of games behind closed doors, but if it's needs must then so be it.

A message of support to the Celtic Family

This is obviously a very worrying time for all of us, and I just want to pass on my thoughts and best wishes to all of our supporters on behalf of all the coaching staff and players here at Celtic. We want everyone to stay safe, to follow the expert advice that has been given and to keep looking after each other and looking out for each other. That's what all of us are doing with our families.

Of course, we're all part of the wider Celtic Family too. It's something that we're all proud of, and everyone at the club appreciates the support our fans always give us. The Celtic Family is a worldwide one, and we know the Celtic fans will continue to show the solidarity and togetherness for which they're renowned throughout football. This is a difficult time for everyone and the priority for all of us is to look after ourselves and to look after each other, but I also know that everyone here at the club is looking forward to when we are able to get back playing in front of our fantastic supporters at Celtic Park. Take care. You'll Never Walk Alone.

On the work of the NHS staff and other key workers
They're putting their lives on the line. This is a virus which is new and there is no ready-made cure for it, and these people are going out there helping to save lives, day in, day out, and putting their own life and health at risk, and it's amazing. Probably things that we took for granted for a long time in our lives has all suddenly changed, and my thoughts and prayers are with them all the way, and the Celtic support would echo that as well. We're hoping that this comes to an end sooner rather than later, and we can get back to some sort of normality for all of us, but these people deserve our unbelievable thanks and gratitude.

On the prospect of completing the season
Everyone at the club – the players, myself, my backroom staff, the fans – want to play the games. Whether that can be achieved or not, that's another thing. It feels like an age away since we played our last game against St Mirren at home, so in terms of keeping the players motivated, keeping them occupied, their own self-motivation is still very, very strong. The only thing they're asking me is when can they get back to training as a group and when can we all start back again, but, obviously, no-one has an answer to that at the minute.

I thought the first half of the season was superb, but

the second half was just as good, particularly domestically. We'd only dropped two points in so many league games and we were making a brilliant challenge again for the Scottish Cup, and we're in the semi-final. But the form that we've been in since the turn of the year was blistering. Even in our last game, we scored five against St Mirren at home, and that was a fine example of the form that we'd had. It's a difficult thing to do at that stage of the season as well, but mentally and physically, they were in a fantastic place. I was delighted with individual performances but also the team as a collective was outstanding.

Defensively, as a unit, we've been functioning great. We even changed the formation and they were very flexible with that as well and adapted to that brilliantly. The football we were playing was fast, free-flowing and we were scoring a lot of goals. I was so pleased with players coming back from injury as well. We actually only had one injury at that stage, which was to Mikey out of the whole group, so in terms of the fitness levels and their appetite for playing, at that stage they had the real bit between their teeth.

The players are the ones who've lost out the most in terms of the opportunity to play in front of the supporters. We're going for nine-in-a-row and a quadruple treble, and I feel sorry for them at this stage, in a footballing sense. Hopefully at some stage it can be started up again, but if not, we'll just have to wait and see what happens and the outcomes of what that is going to be.

NINE
IN A
ROW

Just over two months after the postponement of
the Scottish football calendar, Celtic were declared
Scottish Premiership champions for the ninth
season in a row.

Celtic were 13 points clear at the top of the Premiership with just eight games remaining, and heading inexorably towards a ninth consecutive league title, when the football season came to a halt in the middle of March.

Just over two months later, and with no prospect of the fixtures resuming, the SPFL took the only decision possible and on May 18, 2020 declared Celtic to be the Scottish Premiership champions for 2019/20. It meant that Neil Lennon's side had won nine league titles in a row, replicating the achievement of Jock Stein's legendary side of the 1960s and '70s.

For the Irishman, who had returned to the club under difficult circumstances in February 2019, it was a great achievement and his proudest moment to date as Celtic manager.

He had started the nine-in-a-row run by winning the first three titles, and secured the latest two following the success of Ronny Deila and Brendan Rodgers.

On winning the nine-in-a-row title with Celtic

To be sitting here now as the manager of the nine-in-a-row, and having played a huge part in that, fills me with so much pride. It feels wonderful and I'm so proud of the players. It's an incredible record and to be part of that is something very special, and I think it's thoroughly deserved as well. And also to the fans, in these difficult times, I hope this gives them a huge shot in the arm as well. It's the best, no question it's the best and I've enjoyed the season immensely. I enjoyed the European campaign and winning the League Cup and I enjoyed working with the players every day, I enjoyed working with my staff.

Whether you look at the first half of the season or the second half of the season, we've played some brilliant football throughout, and then you throw in the European campaign, you throw in the League Cup. A lot of that gets overlooked with all that's been going on around Scottish football of late. The style of play pleased me, the amount of goals pleased me, and we had massive contributions from numerous individual players as well.

The cold hard facts are that we were in fantastic form and we were playing very exciting, attacking, free-flowing football, whether that be in the first half of the season or the second half of the season. We had a massive goal difference as well, and from the second half of the season on, the players just kept getting better and better. If you look at this record, it will never be seen again. That's 11 trophies in a row – eleven! That is amazing consistency, amazing desire, amazing talent. They just keep wanting to get better and there's no question that, while other teams were improving this season, we were improving too and the stats show that. I think the right decision has finally come to fruition, and the players can be very proud of their achievements.

On Celtic's swashbuckling football

It's no mean feat to score seven goals at any stage of the season, particularly on the first day when you're still trying to find your best form, so it was a real message that the players meant real business this season. I'm so proud and it's not an easy thing to do – it's only been done a few times in the history of football, and we're sitting here at nine-in-a-row now. It's something that I wanted really badly this season. The league was always the priority and the way the players played, there was a sort of swagger about them, they played some swashbuckling football and that delighted me. The amount of goals we scored delighted me.

There were lots of wee sub stories within the season – Griff coming back, which really pleased me. The new boys bedding in, Frimpong emerging and then the consistency of the likes of Brown, McGregor, Christie, Forrest. And then Edouard at the top of the pitch, who's a very special player. With what's been going on in Scottish football over the last month or so, all these things get forgotten but not by me, certainly not by my staff and I'm sure the fans as well. There's been a lot pressure – a lot of pressure on me, a lot of pressure on the players because everybody wants to beat them, everybody wants to see them fail. People, by nature, get fed up, of seeing the same result all the time but they just won't let that happen. They just have that desire and hunger not to be beaten, and that's why we're sitting here where we are.

On two modern-date Celtic greats

To sit here, quite rightly and justifiably enjoying the fruits of the season, to have won a ninth league title in a row when everyone wants to knock you off your perch, I'm so happy in particular for Scott Brown and James Forrest, because they've been there the whole way through it and that is something very special. They're phenomenal really. I've said it before, but they are two modern-day Celtic greats and they'll be talked about in years to come, if and when they do decide to hang their boots up.

Browny is a great leader, on and off the field. He sets a really high bar, even in training, but he sets the bar the highest when the performances come around and when the games come around. Certainly, he's played a huge part in the success the club's enjoyed over the years.

Jamesy, I'm really proud of him because I gave him his debut and now, 10 years on, he's a nine-in-a-row winner and you look at the achievements he's had over the last five or six years – Player of the Year, International Player of the Year. He was well on course for scoring 20 goals this season and that, for a winger, is a pretty special return. So there was no letting up for either of them really, in terms of their quality and in terms of their consistency of performance, and in terms of their desire to get better.

On the contribution of the backroom staff

John Kennedy does an unbelievable job for me in terms of the organisation and the coaching side of things. Damien Duff was a great partner for him and they forged a real good team together. Stevie Woods has been amazing over the years when you think of the goalkeepers that he's worked with, and he keeps perfecting his craft as well. He's very professional. So that core group of staff has been so essential to me and so important.

Allied to that, the fitness side of things. I think the players have looked really strong this season. When I look back to some of the games this season and how fit they looked, John Currie played a big role in that. I've got a real core of diligent professional staff – I include Jack Nayler in that, and Tim Williamson the physio, so it's a real team effort. Their work ethic is absolutely brilliant and their pride in what they do jumps out at me, and that was really evident when I first took the job on, how professional and diligent and hard-working they are.

It was a help knowing some of the players from my previous time, and you include Mikael Lustig in that as well. But the culture of the club had changed, the social scene had changed, and the professional scene had changed as well, so I had to adapt to that rather than the players adapting to me, especially at a time when we were in March, with only eight games to go in the league. It was crucial that I didn't come in and change too much too soon, or change the way things I wanted them to go, so I had to be very delicate with that and, again, John Kennedy played a big part of that in terms of – he knew the players inside out. We tweaked a few things but the structure and organisation for the players is, relatively, still the same for the players, but the way we wanted to play changed a little bit and we've been successful either way and, again, that's fantastic.

On going for 10-in-a-row

We need the fans right with us, even if it's at a safe distance as it were, on a short-term basis. This is momentous. It comes round once in a lifetime and I want this generation of supporters to be a huge part of that, as they always are. I want them to play their part in it and we'll play our part in entertaining them and making them proud of us. It'll be difficult in the short-term, for the supporters and the players not having each other, working hand in hand, but hopefully that period of time will travel quickly and we can get that togetherness and solidarity back again. This is a generational thing. This team, and certain individuals in this team, have done some really special, incredible things and we want this to be another season to remember. The anticipation is palpable.

What I have to do, as a manager, is keep a lid on

things, get the players in the best condition possible, but I don't think they'll need any extra motivation. And certainly, to have the players and the fans backing us all the way – it's going to be a hell of a ride. When we got the trophy for the nine, I could safely say, it's time to go for the 10 and that's exactly what we're planning on doing.

A lot of people say that players shouldn't need motivation and that is, to a certain extent, true. Players have their own self-motivation, but from a club point of view, from the supporters' point of view and certainly from the group of players, they're going for something that's never been done before and I think that's a huge incentive for them in terms of winning the league. We have to focus them and try not to get too ahead of ourselves, and obviously take each game as it comes, but it's a huge motivation for the players this year, and any new ones coming in – it will be embedded into them very, very quickly what's required.

Post-match notes

Neil Lennon has now won 20 trophies with Celtic — 11 as a player and nine as manager. In his two spells in charge of the team, he has won five league titles, three Scottish Cups and the League Cup, becoming only the second man after Billy McNeill to win all three domestic trophies as a Celtic player and manager.

PLAYER STATS

2019/2020

No.42 CALLUM McGREGOR

	APPS	SUBS	GOALS
League	30	0	9
League Cup	4	0	1
Scottish Cup	2	0	1
Europe	14	0	2
TOTAL	50	0	13

No.8 SCOTT BROWN

	APPS	SUBS	GOALS
League	29	0	2
League Cup	2	1	2
Scottish Cup	3	0	1
Europe	15	0	0
TOTAL	49	1	5

NO.35 KRISTOFFER AJER

	APPS	SUBS	GOALS
League	28	0	3
League Cup	4	0	0
Scottish Cup	2	0	0
Europe	14	1	1
TOTAL	48	1	4

No.49 JAMES FORREST

	APPS	SUBS	GOALS
League	28	0	10
League Cup	2	1	1
Scottish Cup	2	0	0
Europe	14	0	5
TOTAL	46	1	16

No.2 CHRISTOPHER JULLIEN

	APPS	SUBS	GOALS
League	28	0	4
League Cup	3	0	1
Scottish Cup	3	0	0
Europe	11	1	2
TOTAL	45	1	7

No.22 ODSONNE EDOUARD

	APPS	SUBS	GOALS
League	25	2	22
League Cup	2	1	0
Scottish Cup	2	0	0
Europe	13	0	6
TOTAL	42	3	28

No.67 FRASER FORSTER

	APPS	SUBS	GOALS
League	28	0	0
League Cup	2	0	0
Scottish Cup	2	0	0
Europe	7	0	0
TOTAL	39	0	0

No.17 RYAN CHRISTIE

	APPS	SUBS	GOALS
League	17	7	11
League Cup	2	1	0
Scottish Cup	2	0	1
Europe	13	1	7
TOTAL	34	9	19

No.23 BOLI BOLINGOLI

	APPS	SUBS	GOALS
League	14	0	0
League Cup	2	0	0
Scottish Cup	1	0	0
Europe	11	0	0
TOTAL	28	0	0

No.21 OLIVIER NTCHAM

	APPS	SUBS	GOALS
League	17	6	4
League Cup	1	1	2
Scottish Cup	2	0	1
Europe	5	6	1
TOTAL	25	13	8

No.6 NIR BITTON

	APPS	SUBS	GOALS
League	9	6	0
League Cup	1	1	0
Scottish Cup	2	0	0
Europe	6	5	0
TOTAL	18	12	0

No.30 JEREMIE FRIMPONG

	APPS	SUBS	GOALS
League	12	2	2
League Cup	3	0	0
Scottish Cup	1	0	0
Europe	1	0	0
TOTAL	17	2	2

2019/20 Squad stats

No.9 LEIGH GRIFFITHS

	APPS	SUBS	GOALS
League	10	11	9
League Cup	1	0	0
Scottish Cup	2	0	1
Europe	3	4	1
TOTAL	16	15	11

No.27 MOHAMED ELYOUNOUSSI

	APPS	SUBS	GOALS
League	7	3	4
League Cup	3	0	2
Scottish Cup	1	0	0
Europe	5	1	1
TOTAL	16	4	7

No.3 GREG TAYLOR

	APPS	SUBS	GOALS
League	11	1	0
League Cup	0	0	0
Scottish Cup	2	0	0
Europe	2	0	0
TOTAL	15	1	0

No.5 JOZO SIMUNOVIC

	APPS	SUBS	GOALS
League	6	0	1
League Cup	0	0	0
Scottish Cup	0	1	0
Europe	8	1	0
TOTAL	14	2	1

No.19 MIKEY JOHNSTON

	APPS	SUBS	GOALS
League	4	7	2
League Cup	1	1	1
Scottish Cup	0	0	0
Europe	6	2	3
TOTAL	11	10	6

No.33 HATEM ABD ELHAMED

	APPS	SUBS	GOALS
League	3	2	0
League Cup	2	1	0
Scottish Cup	0	0	0
Europe	6	0	0
TOTAL	11	3	0

No.18 TOM ROGIC

	APPS	SUBS	GOALS
League	6	10	2
League Cup	2	0	1
Scottish Cup	1	1	0
Europe	1	1	0
TOTAL	10	12	3

No.16 LEWIS MORGAN

	APPS	SUBS	GOALS
League	3	2	0
League Cup	2	1	0
Scottish Cup	0	0	0
Europe	5	5	2
TOTAL	10	8	2

No.15 JONNY HAYES

	APPS	SUBS	GOALS
League	5	9	1
League Cup	2	2	0
Scottish Cup	0	2	0
Europe	2	4	0
TOTAL	9	17	1

NO.13 MORITZ BAUER

	APPS	SUBS	GOALS
League	6	3	0
League Cup	0	0	0
Scottish Cup	1	0	0
Europe	2	1	0
TOTAL	9	4	0

No.29 SCOTT BAIN

	APPS	SUBS	GOALS
League	2	0	0
League Cup	0	0	0
Scottish Cup	1	0	0
Europe	5	0	0
TOTAL	8	0	0

No.1 CRAIG GORDON

	APPS	SUBS	GOALS
League	0	0	0
League Cup	2	0	0
Scottish Cup	0	0	0
Europe	4	0	0
TOTAL	6	0	0

NO.10 VAKOUN ISSOUF BAYO

	APPS	SUBS	GOALS
League	1	7	0
League Cup	1	0	1
Scottish Cup	0	2	1
Europe	0	5	0
TOTAL	2	14	2

No.11 SCOTT SINCLAIR

	APPS	SUBS	GOALS
League	0	2	0
League Cup	0	1	1
Scottish Cup	0	0	0
Europe	1	3	1
TOTAL	1	6	2

No.11 PATRYK KLIMALA

	APPS	SUBS	GOALS
League	0	2	0
League Cup	0	0	0
Scottish Cup	1	1	0
Europe	0	0	0
TOTAL	1	3	0

No.56 ANTHONY RALSTON

	APPS	SUBS	GOALS
League	0	2	0
League Cup	0	0	0
Scottish Cup	0	0	0
Europe	1	1	0
TOTAL	1	3	0

No.41 SCOTT ROBERTSON

	APPS	SUBS	GOALS
League	0	0	0
League Cup	0	0	0
Scottish Cup	0	0	0
Europe	1	0	0
TOTAL	1	0	0

No.57 STEPHEN WELSH

	APPS	SUBS	GOALS
League	1	0	0
League Cup	0	0	0
Scottish Cup	0	0	0
Europe	0	0	0
TOTAL	1	0	0

No.20 MARIAN SHVED

	APPS	SUBS	GOALS
League	0	1	0
League Cup	0	0	0
Scottish Cup	0	1	0
Europe	0	1	1
TOTAL	0	3	1

No.77 KARAMOKO DEMBELE

	APPS	SUBS	GOALS
League	0	1	0
League Cup	0	0	0
Scottish Cup	0	0	0
Europe	0	1	0
TOTAL	0	2	0

No.14 DANIEL ARZANI

	APPS	SUBS	GOALS
League	0	0	0
League Cup	0	0	0
Scottish Cup	0	1	0
Europe	0	0	0
TOTAL	0	1	0

No.52 EWAN HENDERSON

	APPS	SUBS	GOALS
League	0	0	0
League Cup	0	0	0
Scottish Cup	0	0	0
Europe	0	1	0
TOTAL	0	1	0

No.4 JACK HENDRY

	APPS	SUBS	GOALS
League	0	0	0
League Cup	0	1	0
Scottish Cup	0	0	0
Europe	0	0	0
TOTAL	0	1	0

2019/20 Squad stats

OWN GOALS			
	APPS	**SUBS**	**GOALS**
League	0	0	3
League Cup	0	0	0
Scottish Cup	0	0	0
Europe	0	0	1
TOTAL	0	0	4

TOTALS			
	APPS	**SUBS**	**GOALS**
League	330	86	89
League Cup	44	12	13
Scottish Cup	33	9	6
Europe	176	44	34
TOTAL	583	151	142